Also in The Crafts Series from Little, Brown
Gerald Clow, General Editor

BLACK AND WHITE PHOTOGRAPHY
Henry Horenstein

CROCHET
Mary Tibbals Ventre

POTTERY
Cora Pucci

LEATHERWORK
Benjamin Maleson

WOODWORKING
Raphael Teller

OFF-LOOM WEAVING
Elfleda Russell

STAINED GLASS
Barbara and Gerry Clow

SILVERSMITHING
Nicholas D. Humez

Forthcoming

SUPER 8 PHOTOGRAPHY
Barry Schonhaut

NEEDLEPOINT

A Basic Manual

NEEDLEPOINT

A Basic Manual

CAROL HUEBNER COLLINS

Little, Brown and Company — Boston – Toronto

First Edition

T 05/76

Library of Congress Cataloging in Publication Data

Collins, Carol Huebner.
  Needlepoint: a basic manual.

  (The Little, Brown crafts series)
  Bibliography: p.
  1. Canvas embroidery. I. Title.
TT778.C3C64   746.4'4   76-2695
ISBN 0–316–15225–0

Published simultaneously in Canada by Little, Brown & Company (Canada) Limited

Printed in the United States of America

To my husband and children. Without them, even needlepoint would be no fun at all.

The Husband's Complaint

I've heard of wives too musical — too talkative — too quiet
Of scolding and of gaming wives and those too fond of riot;
But yet of all the errors I know, which to the women fall;
For ever doing fancy work, I think exceeds them all.

The other day when I went home no dinner was for me,
I asked my wife the reason; she answered, "One, two, three,"
I told her I was hungry and stamped upon the floor
She never even looked at me, but murmured "One green more."

If any lady comes to tea, her bag is first surveyed,
And if the pattern pleases her, a copy there is made.
She stares too at the gentlemen, and when I ask her why,
'Tis, "oh my love, the pattern of his waistcoat struck my eye."

Ah! The misery of a working wife, with fancy work run wild;
And hands that never do aught else for husband or for child;
Our clothes are rent, our bills unpaid; my house is in disorder;
And all because my lady wife has taken to embroider.

A History of Needlemaking
M. T. MORRALL, 1852

The Little, Brown Crafts Series is designed and published for the express purpose of giving the beginner — usually a person trained to use his head, not his hands — an idea of the basic techniques involved in a craft, as well as an understanding of the inner essence of that medium. Authors were sought who do not necessarily have a "name" but who thoroughly enjoy sharing their craft, and all their sensitivities to its unique nature, with the beginner. Their knowledge of their craft is vital, although it was realized from the start that one person can never teach all the techniques available.

The series helps the beginner gain a sense of the spirit of the craft he chooses to explore, and gives him enough basic instruction to get him started. Emphasis is laid on creativity, as crafts today are freed from having to be functional; on process, rather than product, for in the making is the finding; and on human help, as well as technical help, as so many prior teaching tools have said only "how" and not "why." Finally, the authors have closed their books with as much information on "next steps" as they could lay their hands on, so that the beginner can continue to learn about the craft he or she has begun.

Gerald Clow

Contents

Introduction

Though it is normally referred to as a craft, I prefer to think of needlepoint as an art. Like the painter, the needlepoint artist works on canvas, but the medium is yarn rather than pigments. The needleworker's objective, like the painter's, is the communication of ideas. This is accomplished through the interplay of fibers, colors, and texture.

Since the early twentieth century needlepoint has consisted, for most practitioners, of a single stitch, variously called the Tent, the Continental, or the Half-Cross stitch. Usually this stitch has been worked on backgrounds of pre-designed canvas. This approach to the art has stunted the imaginations and numbed the minds of too many needlepointers while developing their infinite patience. How needlepoint ever survived such narrow definition is a miracle!

Happily, we are now in an era in which needlepoint is regaining the freedom it enjoyed in earlier centuries when every stitch possible was used, colors abounded, imaginations took flight, and few stopped to worry about their true worth as artists. Indeed, there was a time in the history of the art when needlework was so rich and copious that laws were enacted to limit the amount of needlework allowed on clothing and household decoration.

We have regained that earlier freedom at a moment when needlepoint is beginning to advance toward a new art form. Today's needlepoint practitioners are not letting their ideas be straitjacketed by convention. We no longer feel compelled to cover every intersection of the canvas with yarn. We are willing to experiment with new fibers, unusual techniques, and objects never before connected with needlepoint.

Modern science is furnishing us new materials with still-unknown potential, which offer new qualities for expressing our ideas. We're merrily cutting holes in canvases, adding strange objects, creating a new art form that is strictly contemporary.

Because I feel that one cannot soar until one learns to fly, I've planned this text so it begins with the very first steps. It will be useful, I hope, to those who have never felt the joy of holding a threaded needle, never planned and executed a project, never dabbled with new concepts and techniques as a needlepoint artist.

My objective in writing this book has been to create a textbook for teachers and students who want such an aid to learning — a text, I hope, that brings together in one volume all that can be introduced into a classroom to make needlepoint a live and enticing subject. Those lucky enough to be able to learn solely from the written work, will I hope, find this book an inspiration to begin to develop their own ideas. Since there are more than four hundred stitches, with more being "invented" every day, I have not tried to cover them all. Basic stitches are included in this volume. There are numerous stitch encyclopedias on the market for the adventurous needlepointer; the method of working them all is the same as I expound here.

Since it's hard to know where one is going if we don't know where we've been, I also have included a short history of needlepoint.

As you begin this book, I have only one bit of advice: relax, have fun, and enjoy the time you'll spend creating beauty. And if you don't like the results, you can always rip out your work and start over — there's no such thing in needlepoint as an irremediable mistake. Not many things worth doing in life are so forgiving.

Acknowledgments

My deepest gratitude goes to: my husband, for his constant support and for contributing his literary talent to organize my over-enthusiastic words; my children, for their love and patience in taking over my housewifely duties while I slaved over a hot typewriter; my many students, who have taught me as much as I have taught them, for their encouragement, their joy, and their willingness to lend their sampler pillows for the photographs.

Also to Norma Meehan, whose wizardry with pen and ink makes my ideas seem real. And to Gary Mills, for translating my thoughts into photographic art.

To Doris Levanthal, Lynn Cassady, and Mary Lou Comstock, for advice and professional opinions and time spent beyond the call of friendship. And to Suzanne Sheehan for sharing her needlework so generously.

And especially to Chottie Alderson, who taught me that ideas do have wings if we but have the courage to try — and who introduced me to the techniques necessary to accomplish this flight.

part

I

History and Materials

Chapter 1
A History of Needlepoint

Needlework was one of the earliest accomplishments of man. Fragments of a rug found in an Egyptian tomb have been carbon-dated to 5000 B.C. The art of needlework in some form has been known and revered at least since then.

According to the Roman historian Pliny the Elder, who lived in the first century A.D., the Phrygians were the first people to use a needle to embroider material. In those times, needles were made from bones, quills, or bronze. Steel needles were not invented until the sixteenth century.

Canvas, as it is known today, was not invented until the early 1800s. Before that, needlepoint was done on even-weave linen and was often referred to as "counted thread work." As such, it was a category of embroidery rather than a distinct art form.

There are numerous references in ancient writings, especially in the Bible, to copiously decorated materials, to gold and silver embroidery on priestly robes, tabernacle veils, and clothing in general.

When Menelaus took Helen home from Troy after the Trojan war, they stopped in Egypt, whose rulers presented Helen with an embroidery basket as a token of their esteem, just as our heads of state today exchange gifts. The very sails on the ancient ships were embroidered; that was how ships were identified before flags were developed.

The earliest embroidery was done in silk. It is said that a Chinese empress discovered silk one day when she accidentally dropped a cocoon into her cup of tea and the heat loosened the binding between the silk threads. Whether you want to accept that story or not, there is no question about the earliest needlepoint being done in China, where it was known for years as the forbidden stitch — because it was worked on such fine backgrounds, with such minute stitches, that many practitioners went blind from their work.

Needlepoint has always been associated with the worship of gods and with nobility. Special items were made to be offered to the Greek gods, and for centuries needlework was exclusively the occupation and the right of the wealthy and ruling classes. The Bayeaux tapestry, traditionally reputed to have been worked in the eleventh century by Matilda, wife of William the Conquerer, is a prime example; it commemorated the conquest of England by the Normans.

For centuries, the only stitch used in what we now term needlepoint was the Tent stitch, a quiet, simple stitch that covers diagonally one intersection of canvas, quite versatile and unassuming, and possessing little texture. As world travel developed, new stitches were introduced, new patterns were copied, and new yarns and techniques spread. The Crusades contributed significantly to the widespread dispersal of techniques and patterns. It was also about that time that needlework stopped being strictly for church use and began to serve domestic uses as well. Designs continued to have a religious flavor, however, for a long time.

The East India Company exerted enormous influence on the art of needlework. East India was trading all over the world at the time the steel needle was invented; simultaneously, the era of Henry VIII in England and the Reformation in Europe were accelerating the trend for needlework to be considered part of the domestic as well as the ecclesiastical domain. It was a flamboyant age that knew no bounds, and this was reflected in the needlework of the times.

The Tree of Life, an Indian design, was brought to England at about this time. It entranced English needleworkers. The homes of the nobility were heavy, stone mansions, filled with solid oak furniture. Many tapestries were required to hold the heat in cold, stone-walled rooms in winter. Many chair coverings and pillows — a contemporary idea — were required to make the furniture more attractive and comfortable. These materials were covered, every inch, with needlework, and the Tree of Life was the favorite design. The Tree of Life design consists of one tree trunk growing upward from hillocks; the tree has many branches, each bearing an abundance of different kinds of flowers and fruits. True to the tenor of the times, the hillock represented worldly troubles and the tree symbolized man's growing and looking to God to overcome his troubles. The fruits and flowers signified the abundance of graces which God showered upon man. The design is still popular today, although its symbolism is largely forgotten.

During the reign of Elizabeth I in England, a man's station in life was signalled by the amount of decoration on his clothing. The wealthier he was, the more leisure time his wife had, and the more serving girls he could afford, to embroider his finery. Eventually, clothing became so overladen with decoration that laws were passed limiting the amount of embroidery permitted in English households and designating those who could wear it.

The greatest period for the needle arts in England — the *Opus Anglicanum* — had been the century from about 1250 to 1350. The Black Death, wars, and the increased manufacture of materials brought that era to an end. The William and Mary period (1689–1702) and the Queen Anne period (1702–1714) were perhaps the zenith for domestic needlework.

Needlepoint kits as we know them today were introduced in 1803. A Mr. Philipson of Berlin first got the idea of copying the works of the old masters (Leonardo, Raphael, etc.) on graph paper. He allotted one stitch to each square of the graph. By following his chart, the needlepointer worked the stitches in the colors indicated and reproduced the masterpiece. The concept was similar to that of today's "paint by number" sets. Simultaneously, new dyes were developed in Berlin which produced more and brighter varieties of yarn. The kits — which included the new "Berlin yarns" and Mr. Philipson's graphs — became known as "Berlin work" and were popular during the pre-Victorian and Victorian eras. Many of these projects still exist. The kits used only the Tent stitch, since it is the most versatile for working small areas of canvas.

With progress in the textile field which enabled machines to copy any pattern onto material, and with increased urbanization and shifts in values away from craftsmanship, needlework went into eclipse toward the end of the nineteenth century, lasting into the twentieth. Needlepointers relied almost entirely on the unexciting Tent stitch, forgetting many lovely pattern stitches that had been current a century before. Not until the 1920s were texture stitches resurrected, and not until the 1960s did they regain a wide measure of acceptance. It was as though there had been a complete rift in the development of needlework, and everything had to be learned anew.

Today, we are passing resolutely out of the "just fill the background" era of needlepoint — and high time! The 1970s are abundantly blessed with good designers offering outstanding patterns to be worked. Still in the minority are those who create their own innovative designs. That, as I will have occasion to observe in the pages ahead, is for the future.

Chapter 2
The Materials of Needlepoint

All you really need to do needlepoint are three things: canvas, yarn, and needles. Add a waterproof marking pen if you'd like to design your own canvas. There are a variety of other supplies and materials on the market that sometimes add ease and comfort to the working of the canvas, and, if you like, you can spend a great deal of money on them. But they are not prerequisites to a beautiful project.

Canvas

Canvas is an open-mesh scrim, the underlying base upon which the wool is worked to form a new fabric.

There is a great variety of canvas on the market today. It comes in various numbers of holes to the inch, in various widths, and in greatly varying quality. The aid of a knowledgeable, reliable shopowner is invaluable until you know your way around.

Prices vary both with the quality and the width of the canvas. Although it can be purchased in a 27-inch width, the more standard canvas widths are 36 and 40 inches, and a judicious selection between those two widths can provide you with enough material for two or more projects. As far as length is concerned, you can buy canvas by the inch, the partial yard, or the yard.

Poor quality canvas is a waste of money and time. Finished projects are capable of lasting several lifetimes if the material is of good quality. Canvas of poor quality will add frustrations and disappointments to your work. Since there is little difference in price between poor and good quality canvas, do get the best.

A good quality canvas is smooth with a polished weave. Unfortunately, even good canvas may have a few knots or "patched" areas. It is impossible to get any canvas without a few knots, but those on good material are fewer and smaller and will be on the back side of the canvas. Should you encounter a large knot that interferes with your needlework, the offending threads can be removed and rewoven with a thread taken from the edge of the canvas. The new thread will follow the interlacing of the old one exactly.

Canvas can be made of linen, cotton, nylon, or plastic. Linen is the very best, but it's also expensive and almost impossible to find today. Cotton is usually good and will offer the largest choice at most shops. Both linen and cotton canvas consist of threads interwoven and then heavily sized. The very cheapest grades are starched rather than sized and are greatly inferior in quality. These are best avoided.

Nylon canvas is relatively new on the market and offers numerous possibilities. It is much more pliable than regular canvas and therefore makes an excellent choice for clothing. However, it will not block back into shape once it gets out of shape while being worked, so a frame to hold the canvas is a wise investment for this particular medium. Plastic "canvas" is also fairly new. It is useful for certain kinds of projects which require rigidity, such as purses.

Whatever the basic material, needlepoint canvas comes in two types, called mono and Penelope.

Mono canvas consists of single threads running horizontally and vertically. Mono is easily worked and much more gentle on the eyesight than Penelope. A new weave, called interlocked canvas, has recently been introduced which remedies the drawback of unlocked canvas — namely, that the threads of unlocked canvas tend to "roam" with the pressure of the stitch. A few stitches cannot be used on such canvas. With the canvas threads locked, however, all stitches can be used. There remain times, as in pulled work, when unlocked canvas is the best choice. This kind of canvas can also be sewn lightly to a woven material to provide a grid for embroidering a design on the material; when the embroidery is completed, the canvas threads can be removed with tweezers, leaving the design on the woven material.

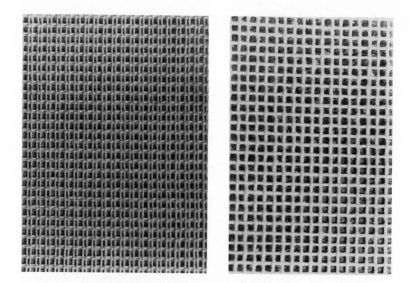

#10 Penelope (left) compared to #10 mono canvas

Penelope canvas has two threads placed side by side on both the horizontal and vertical axes. It is also known as double-thread or double-mesh canvas. Its main asset is that it can be subdivided into areas to allow four small stitches to be worked in place of two larger stitches, thus permitting more detail to be worked in parts of a design.

Penelope canvas is supposedly named for Penelope, wife of Ulysses, who would weave all day and unravel her work all night. This canvas was originally quite flimsy and used in place of mono to work patterns on uneven-weave materials; it was pulled out when the work was completed, as described in the paragraph above.

Using #12 Penelope canvas, the threads of the Penelope are separated for the fireplug's face and the butterfly, giving twenty-four stitches to an inch and permitting more detail. Surrounding the petit point are twelve stitches to the inch.

#3 rug canvas and #10 needlepoint canvas

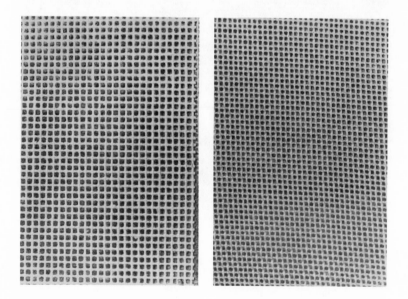

#14 needlepoint canvas and #18 petit-point canvas

Canvas comes in various sizes, distinguished by numbers which indicate the number of threads (and therefore potential stitches) per inch. Double-mesh, or Penelope, is characterized by two numbers, such as 10/20, 12/24, and so forth.

Quick-point, which is worked on canvas containing from three to eight threads per inch (#3 through #8), is used for jobs you want to finish quickly but which demand little detail. This size canvas is sometimes known as rug canvas, because its original use was in making rugs. To fill it, you'll need either rug yarn or three to four full strands of Persian yarn in the needle.

Needlepoint canvas, which contains 10 to 16 threads per inch (#10 through #16), is the most commonly used material for needlepoint projects. The work fills up rather quickly on this size canvas, yet much more detail is possible than in quick-point. Most pre-designed, commercially packaged kits are worked on #10 or #12 mesh canvas. Number 13 is known as Bargello canvas; #14 is all-around utility canvas.

Petit point is worked on canvas containing 18 to 40 threads per inch. To get an idea of how fine #40 canvas would be, take a look at some nylon hose; that's woven with about 40 threads to the inch. Needless to say, fine meshes provide for a great deal of detail. Usually only one ply of yarn (one strand of Persian yarn has three plies, which can be separated) is needed in petit-point work. Silk or DMC embroidery floss is often used in this kind of fine work. Since the floss closely resembles silk when worked, it provides elegant effects at less expense.

The number of the canvas you choose will be determined by the project at hand. Rug canvas is obviously unsuitable for a small box top, while petit point would be far too tedious for a rug or a wall hanging. The amount of detail required in the project offers another guide to proper canvas size. Weigh the detail required against the amount of work it will take to complete the project in a reasonable amount of time — unless you are the rare needlepointer for whom time is no object. When in doubt, #12 or #14 canvas is a good choice. If some detail is needed but the job is large, double-mesh canvas could solve the problem, since it has the flexibility of offering spots of detail where they may be needed in the design, along with faster work where detail is not needed. If double-mesh canvas is not available, another size canvas can be appliquéd to the work to provide detail. (More will be said about this technique in Chapter 14.)

Yarn

Wool, a natural fiber with a unique resiliency, is the desired yarn for most needlepoint. It comes in a host of colors and varieties, and each variety has its uses. Only one quality is universal to all needlepoint and crewel yarns — the way in which they are spun gives them the desirability and durability for heirloom work.

Wool is taken from sheep in dirty lumps. Washing and carding (combing with steel brushes) turn the

lumps into balls and strands of fiber, which are then spun together into lengths. A wool thread used for needlework will be spun very long and thin. Such threads may be 24 inches long. Several threads are then twisted together to make a usable strand. Not only thread length but fiber length is important. Some yarns are tightly twisted but have short fibers; these are less desirable for needlework than long-fibered yarn.

Knitting wool, in contrast to needlework wool, is normally spun short (about four inches per thread) and fat, so that a new puff of wool must be added about every four inches or so to obtain any length in the strand. This is why knitting wool tends to shred and pull apart when it's used for needlework.

However, knitting wool can be used for special effects if it suits the purpose of a project. So can a lot of other things — man-made yarn, angora, string, or rope, for example. But they are harder to use and don't wear as well as yarns spun especially for needlework. They should be cut into short lengths, around 12 inches at most to wear best.

Some kits are now including acrylic yarn which closely resembles wool yarn in appearance. Like nylon canvas, this yarn cannot be blocked back once it is pulled out of shape. Again, I recommend a frame.

There are several metallic — gold and silver — threads made for needlework which wear well and resist rust or tarnish. Such materials are excellent for highlights. If they are too thick to be pulled through the holes of the canvas, lay them on top and tack them down with invisible thread. These yarns ravel quite easily while being worked. To avoid frustration and losing a good portion of the thread, tie a small knot in each end. The thread will be harder to work for about three stitches, but it soon becomes easier.

Wool needlepoint yarn comes in two types, known as tapestry and Persian.

Tapestry yarn is indivisible. It has a uniform thickness which can be used only on #10 or #12 canvas. It is too thick for #14 and too thin to cover well on #8. Two threads together might cover #3 or #5 canvas, however. Color selection is limited but beautiful with tapestry yarn. Not so long ago, this style of yarn was the only kind available.

Persian yarn comes in three plies and is divisible. A full, three-ply strand is the same thickness as tapestry yarn. The advantage of Persian yarn is that the plies can be divided or added to in order to make the yarn fit the canvas of your choice. True Persian yarn actually has three strands of two-ply yarn. Only one or two manufacturers make a true Persian, although many companies make Persian-type yarn. Some of them, unfortunately, are of too poor a quality to warrant use. You may have to do some trial-and-error experimentation with Persian-type yarn unless you deal with a good, reliable shop. There are four hundred or more colors available in Persian yarns, and this type of yarn is now being used as an all-purpose material. One ply works well in crewel work, while three or four full strands can be used for rug-making. Originally, in fact, Persian yarn was developed for rugs; only recently has its use broadened to other projects.

Persian (above) and tapestry wool

Yarn is dyed in lots, one dyeing creating a single dye lot. It is best to buy enough yarn from one dye lot for an entire project, as there may be subtle changes in color between one lot and another. However, if it is necessary to use some yarn from a different dye lot that doesn't exactly match, you can use one strand from each lot in the needle at the same time, which will blend the two shades together and minimize the color difference.

Estimating the amount of yarn needed for a project can be tricky, and here again the advice of a good shop person is helpful. It is much better, as a general rule, to overbuy and use the remnants in another project than to run the risk of having to match colors should you run out.

The best way to determine the amount of yarn needed is to work a square-inch swatch of the stitch to be used; measure the amount of yarn needed and then multiply this amount by the number of square inches in the project. Even then, dividing the yarn requirements among the various colors can present problems.

Here's a mathematical approach to estimating:

#10 canvas: number of sq. in. x 1½ = number of 33-inch strands

#14 canvas: number of sq. in. x 4 ÷ 3 = number of 33-inch strands

#18 canvas: number of sq. in. x 2 ÷ 3 = number of 33-inch strands

Yarn is usually bought by weight. Thus, 44 strands, 33 inches long, equal approximately an ounce of yarn. But weight is affected by humidity;

therefore it's better to count strands to assure desired coverage and weight than to use a scale.

Large quantities of yarn can be purchased in hanks. When untwisted and opened into a large circle, the hank is cut through the end that has the knot, thus creating strands 66 inches long. When cut into halves, the strands are the standard 33 inches.

The quality of yarn determines the price. Like canvas, yarn is no place to save money. Not only does the wearing quality of yarn vary with price, so does the working quality. Cheaper yarns tend to fuzz, thin out, and break quickly with the wear caused by pulling them through the holes of the canvas. Cutting such yarns into shorter lengths will alleviate that problem.

Needles

Tapestry needles come with large eyes and blunt ends. To determine the right size needle for your project, choose one that falls easily through the holes of the canvas but also has an eye large enough to hold the amount of thread you'll need to cover the canvas. Normally you'll match these needle sizes with the corresponding canvas numbers:

Canvas	Needle
#3–5	= 13
#10–12	= 18–19
#14–16	= 20–21
#18–24	= 23–24

Floor frame

Optional Equipment

There is all sorts of additional equipment on the market to entice the needleworker, ranging from near-necessities to fancy frills.

Frames have been used for needlework projects since the Middle Ages; although needlepoint frames have been out of favor for most of this century, there are signs that they are making a comeback. My opinion is that they are necessities. I find them useful for nearly all projects except those too small to go on a frame.

The main advantage of frames is that they keep the canvas taut and straight, so that even the most hard-headed diagonal stitch won't pull the material out of shape. Held properly, a frame leaves both hands free for stitching — one below and one above the piece — and the work goes much faster.

The ideal frame has top and bottom rollers to which are stapled strips of heavy cotton tape. The rollers are separated by side bars to stretch the canvas taut. The canvas is sewn to the tapes and is rolled on the rollers as the work progresses. Some frames come with a set of three sizes of rollers and one set of side bars. The whole contraption resembles a small quilting frame.

There are lap frames, table frames, and floor frames. All have advantages and should be chosen according to personal preference. Needlepoint frames are always rectangular, not round, and wider than the work. Round frames, useful for crewel embroidery, crimp the work, causing creases which

and lap frame

may not come out; they also tend to draw the work crooked, which is what we're attempting to avoid in the first place.

Artist's stretchers or old picture frames can be used in place of frames. Depending on the kind of project at hand, these frames can be left in place when the work is finished.

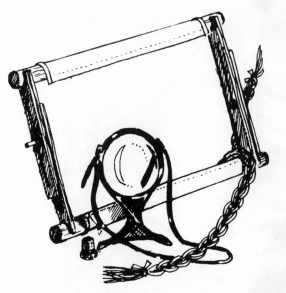

Magnifying glasses are useful for fine work. There is a style that hangs around the neck, the base resting on the chest, which works well for petit point. Magnifying spectacles of the sort available at the five-and-dime store are the preference of some needleworkers.

The waterproof marking pen is more an essential of the needleworker's tools than a luxury. Such pens are useful in creating your own designs. Remember that when the work is finished, you'll be using water to block it. If the marking tool is not waterproof, the design marks may bleed through the yarn and mar your work. If that should happen, your only recourse will be to take out the damaged yarn and replace it — not a very pleasant job.

Today only Nepo brand pens have been proven waterproof. Some markers are called "permanent" but, because of sizing in the canvas, will bleed in the blocking process. If you have doubt about the waterproof qualities of a pen, dampen a piece of paper toweling and dab a mark on the edge to see if it bleeds. Even this test is not foolproof, because paper toweling, unlike canvas, has no sizing. The towel test, however, is useful when you buy painted canvases; the paint isn't always waterproof, no matter what the price, and may bleed onto the yarn during blocking.

If you have reservations about the waterproof quality of ink, spray it with a clear acrylic spray obtainable at any hobby shop; this will set the ink so that it's safe to use.

Ball-point pens are seldom if ever waterproof. A pencil is also dangerous to use because the graphite (which is what pencil "lead" really is) tends to rub off on the yarn as it is being worked. Graphite has also been known to eat away the canvas over the years.

You can use acrylic or oil paints to paint a canvas, but they should be thinned so that they cover the canvas but don't fill in the holes. Enough time must be allowed for them to dry thoroughly before any work is begun.

Braiding yarn loosely makes a very convenient method of keeping the yarn together and at one's fingertips. Using a twist tie from the end of a bread wrapper, tie all of the yarn together at one end. Braid it loosely and apply another twist tie at the other end. These braids can then be attached to a shower-curtain ring so that they are kept together. One strand may be pulled out of a braid at a time without displacing the rest of the yarn until the yarn is almost used up.

Do not store yarn while it is braided for any length of time; when stored for months or years, the yarn will tend to become permanently kinked and will mar any project it is used on. When storing it after the project is finished, unbraid it and tie it loosely into a knot.

Lovely yarn caddies, made of wood finished to match your furniture, are available to hold yarn. Other methods of keeping yarn separated and handy include covering clothes hangers with material and attaching small rings around the bottom to hold yarn; tying yarn onto embroidery hoops, and using special "artist's palettes" to hold the yarn.

Needleworkers are well advised to use the lowly thimble; it can save you from a pricked finger. Another safety tip is to put a cork on the end of the scissors when they are not in use. Medicine bottles make fine storage places for needles. And a bright ribbon strung through the handles of the scissors lets them hang around your neck so they'll be handy when you need them.

part

II

Projects

Samplers

Chapter 3
Sampler Stitch Diagrams

Years ago, everyone made samplers. Before design books were easily accessible, the sampler itself was the needleworker's own textbook. Any pleasing design the craftsperson wanted to remember went into the sampler, where it could be copied and shared for a lifetime and longer.

After design books began to be published, samplers became practice-stitch cloths. Little girls not yet of school age were given samplers to do to keep their fingers busy and their minds free, and to help them develop coordination and artistic ability.

Today's samplers often combine both purposes. They offer the needleworker a good place to practice stitches until they are mastered. They also offer a record of stitch design and characteristics.

A good sampler can be made with an 18-inch square of #14 mono canvas, about five ounces of Persian-type yarn in four to five colors, and a #20 tapestry needle. These materials will yield a 14-inch pillow, so colors should be chosen that will complement the room in which the end product will be placed.

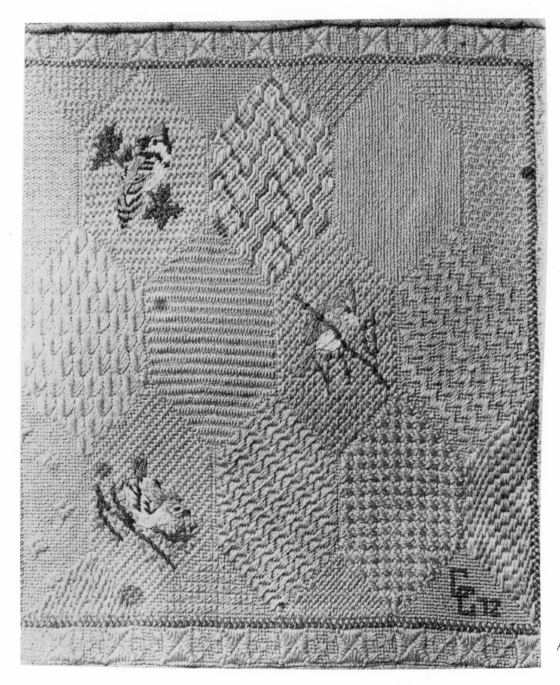

A geometric design

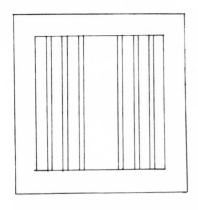

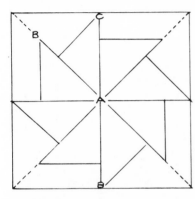

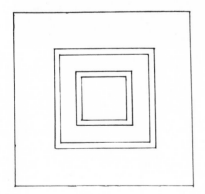

Three approaches to sampler design

You may find it takes more time to design a sampler — or any other project you undertake — than it does to do the work. A piece of brown paper (an unfolded grocery sack is quite adequate) is recommended to begin your designing, since the paper is cheap and expendable.

First draw a 14-inch square on the paper, then subdivide the square into the same number of areas as there are stitches to be worked in your sampler. Sixteen is a good number, but you may find it an oversimplification simply to divide the area into 16 squares. You'll seldom want to work any pattern in squares alone, and this is a good time to learn how to coordinate shapes. Squares also present a basic dullness of design which is difficult to overcome.

Ideas for designs can come from geometric shapes, from quilt patterns, from your personal interests, or from family pleasures. For example, if you lay leaves from various kinds of trees over the design area and then use fall colors, you can create a stunning pattern. Birds can be embroidered in areas to represent the species that spend the winter at your bird feeder. Flowers, animals, mushrooms, and many other commonplace objects can be incorporated into patterns.

You don't have to subdivide your area evenly and probably shouldn't. There ought to be two relatively large areas to enclose Bargello patterns, and these should be balanced not only against each other but against the rest of the design, so that the whole has a pleasing, flowing pattern.

Sketch your pattern ideas on pieces of paper until

you come up with a design that satisfies you. Then trace over the lines of the final design with the darkest ink possible, so that the lines are clear and distinct.

An alternative to expendable brown paper is layout or tracing paper. If your first design needs some improvement, another sheet can be laid over the original and modified without having to redesign the entire pattern.

Now you're ready to transfer the design to the canvas. Canvas is sheer; the lines of your design can be seen quite clearly through the canvas when the design paper is placed underneath it. Sometimes putting a light under the paper and canvas makes things clearer; you can use an artist's lamp or a light table, or you can tape the design paper and canvas to a window and use daylight as a light source.

With a Nepo waterproof marking pen, trace your design on the canvas. Center the 14-inch design square on the 18-inch canvas so that a 2-inch border of canvas is left all around the design for seam allowance. Take care that all straight lines are marked on a straight row of holes. Some canvas is woven with distortions, but the rows will straighten out when you block the work, so keep your holes in a row. Working diagonal lines on diagonal holes will save you headaches later on, but it isn't absolutely essential. Circles will be optical illusions; try one and you'll see what I mean.

The edges of the canvas should be taped with masking tape or bias tape stitched on the edges. Or the edges can be turned under and stitched. The

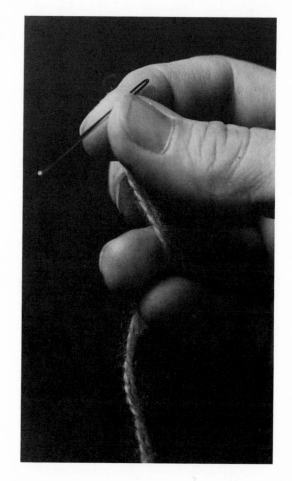

Threading the needle

reason for this step is that canvas tends to ravel severely, and if you don't tape, you could end several weeks of work on a project with a deep fringe on four sides. Untaped edges also tend to catch the yarn as it is worked, making the sampler unnecessarily fuzzy and weak.

Threading the needle is a tricky process. You have to persuade the yarn, which seems to have a tendency at such moments to become thick and fat, to go through the tiny eye of the needle. Some days, turning the trick seems to call for magic. Here's a tip: Fold about two inches of yarn over the needle, catching the ends between the little finger and a ring finger. Pull down firmly to put tension on the yarn; this will flatten it a bit. Now place the needle and the yarn between the pads of your thumb and first finger (not the fingernails!) and squeeze the yarn still flatter. Next, pull the needle out gently without disturbing the yarn. If you've done it right, you shouldn't see any yarn at this point; it is being firmly squeezed between the pads of the fingers. Gently and slowly roll the fingers apart until just the barest hint of yarn filaments and color can be seen. The bulk of the yarn is still being squeezed between your fingers. Push the needle gently down over the filaments and between the fingers; keep the fingers firm. When even a few hairs have been caught into the needle's eye, the rest can be pulled through with ease.

When all else fails, there are needle threaders. But they have a way of getting lost when you need them. Try to learn to thread the needle as described above.

It takes practice, to be sure, but after a short time you'll be threading everything this way, even sewing thread.

Yarn has minute hairs which virtually require a microscope to see. For neat work, it is wise to lay these hairs down rather than fluffing them up in working the piece. To determine which way you want the yarn to go through the canvas holes, pick up a strand of yarn in both hands (thumb and first fingers next to each other in the center of the strand). Pull gently toward each end; try to tell which has a rougher feel. Put the needle on the end of the rough direction.

I might add that modern spinning methods make it impossible sometimes to tell which direction is rough and which smooth. Then, of course, the needle can go on either end of the yarn.

Chapter 4

Stitches

Everything up until now has been, in a sense, preliminary. You have your yarn, canvas, needles. You've designed a sampler. Now you're ready to put it all together to create the finished needlepoint project. To do that, you need to know stitches.

The number and variety of needlepoint stitches approaches infinity, but you needn't master every last one. The following pages will explain and illustrate twenty-one of the most important and basic stitches — plus some variations. They will get you comfortably through any project you might undertake. Many additional stitches are nothing more than other variations on these twenty-one. As you become more accomplished, you will find it easy to pick up new stitches from other needlepointers, other books, classes, and your own imagination.

The only way to chart stitches, I'm afraid, is by using numbers. Numbers are necessary evils. Each stitch has a rhythm of its own, however, and you ought to try to learn the rhythm and not depend on

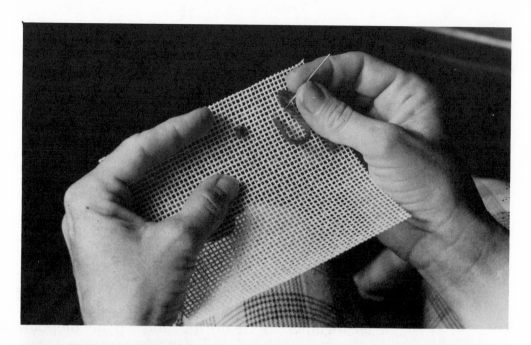

the numbers. Sooner or later, after all, you'll come to the end of the numbers, but the stitch goes on. Knowing the rhythm of the stitch will help you remember it, enlarge on it, or modify it.

Any stitch described here may be used anyplace on your sampler, except in the two large areas of your design which are reserved for the Bargello stitch. Be sure, also, to plan your initials and the date in the design — either in the center, as an accent point, or on an edge, in which case they will probably be smaller.

In applying stitches, with few exceptions you should draw the needle from back to front (that is, toward you) on the odd numbers and from front to back (away from you) on the even numbers.

The correct method of stitching requires two distinct movements. First pull the needle forward, tugging all of the yarn through the hole, and then push the needle back away from you, again pulling all the yarn through. This may seem slow and cumbersome, and you'll probably be tempted at first to use a scooping or sewing motion. Resist the temptation. Doing it correctly will produce smoother stitches, better yarn tension, clearer patterns, and less risk of canvas distortion. Though faster, scooping results in uneven tension and a distorted canvas that will be almost impossible to straighten in the blocking process.

Stitches are begun and ended by working the yarn through the back of previously worked areas. Obviously, you can't do that when you are starting out in a clear area and there are no other stitches nearby.

A "waste knot" is laid on top of the canvas an inch or so in the direction that the work will progress. This holds the end of yarn tightly under the canvas so that the stitches will cover it completely on the back side. When the stitching reaches the waste knot, cut it off and pull ends to back of canvas.

Here you'll use a "waste knot" — the only knot used in needlepoint. The knot is tied on the end of the thread and positioned on the top side of the canvas about an inch from the starting point in the direction in which the work will progress. With the yarn running under the canvas, start the stitching at the chosen point and, as you move forward, cover all the yarn on the "tail" up to the knot. When you reach the knot, clip it off, pull the ends to the back, and continue working.

When you finish a length of yarn, work the end under the back of the stitches and clip any that is left over. Always keep the back neatly clipped; these tiny ends have a maddening way of working up to the front of your sampler and spoiling the area.

A good general rule to keep in mind: whenever possible, bring the needle up through an empty hole and push it down through a shared hole (one which already contains a stitch from another row). This alleviates problems of split yarn.

For your sampler, choose as many stitches as you like from those described in this chapter. Work each in the color or colors of your choice; it will help to lay strands of yarn on the sampler areas to determine the basic color scheme before beginning to stitch. Try to balance diagonal stitches with horizontal ones, bright colors with dull, and dark colors with light. Your only constraint is to achieve a pleasing overall result.

Canvas will ravel, even the interlocked varieties. For any project, therefore, that requires stitching or nailing in the finishing stages (such as chair covers or pillows), you are well advised to add two or three rows of Continental stitch outside the finished area to act as a seam allowance. An additional advantage of the extra rows is that they will provide a smooth line to follow when you're stitching. And for beginners, these rows offer an excellent place to begin stitchery where a mistake won't show.

In working these extra rows, do the horizontal rows at top and bottom first. When working the side rows, resist the temptation to turn the project a quarter turn; that would make the stitches lie in the wrong direction. Instead, begin at the top and work down a side, laying each stitch below the one above rather than across. Then turn the canvas so that the bottom is at the top and work down the second vertical row. Turn again for the third row. This technique will lay the stitch in the correct direction without adding any unnecessary yarn to the back side.

At the edge of each segment of your design, you may have to resort to partial stitches. In a partial stitch, the yarn lies just as it would to make a full stitch, but the needle is dropped through the hole at the edge of the pattern, making the stitch shorter than normal. The result should make it appear that the pattern continues but that another area has been placed on top of it, hiding it from sight.

Partials may be confusing at first. The beginner is advised to work the entire area and then go back and fill in the partials after the rhythm of the stitch has been mastered.

Now the stitches.

Half-Cross stitch

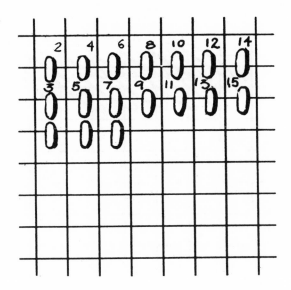

front

Half-Cross stitch

Materials: #14 Penelope canvas; 2-ply strands. Two strands (33 inches long) will cover one square inch.

Uses: Pictures, and anything not receiving stress or constant use; good for shading and fine detail.

Remarks: This stitch has little backing and cannot take wear; cannot be used on mono canvas, and distorts canvas considerably.

Important: Each row is worked from left to right, therefore the canvas must be turned a full 180 degrees at the end of each row to begin a new row. After the first row, the beginning of the stitch will come up through a shared hole (that is, yarn from the last row will already be in the hole); the third row will begin in an empty hole.

back

actual size

Continental stitch

Materials: #14 mono canvas; 2-ply strands. Three strands (33 inches long) will cover one square inch.

Uses: Initials; designs requiring only one or two stitches of a color; any project in the basic stitch.

Remarks: This stitch wears well; can be used on any canvas; and distorts canvas considerably when used in large areas.

Important: Canvas must be turned 180 degrees to begin each row (see Half-Cross); always work rows from right to left.

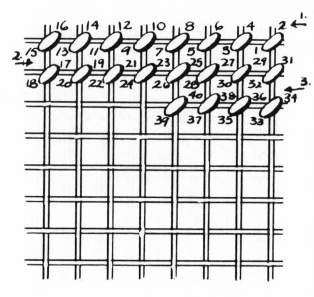

front

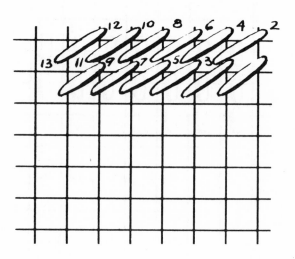

Continental — back

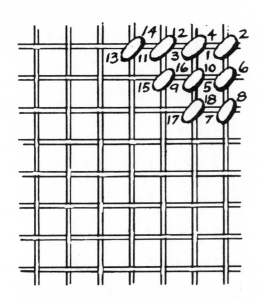

front

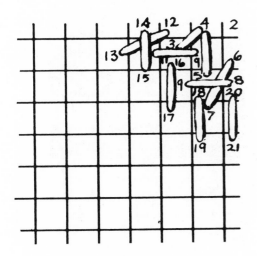

Basketweave — back

Basketweave stitch

Materials: #14 mono canvas; 2-ply strands. Three strands (33 inches long) will cover one square inch.

Uses: Backgrounds; any project requiring strength and wearability. Gives smooth and unassuming texture.

Remarks: This stitch wears extremely well; does not require turning canvas; and does not distort canvas.

Important: No two rows should be worked in the same direction. Stop in the middle of a row, or mark (lightly) the direction of the next stitch to be taken, when ending a working session with this stitch. Begin and end threads horizontally or vertically, never diagonally. Ridges in the work can be caused by failure to apply either of these two rules.

Canvas is woven with the horizontal thread on top first, then the vertical. If care is taken when beginning the Basketweave stitch always to lay the yarn over the top canvas thread, the direction of the stitch is easily determined.

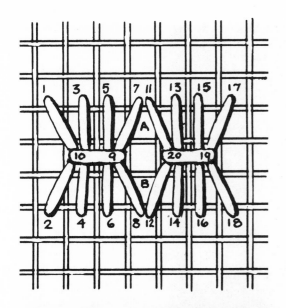

Sheaf (or Shell) stitch

Materials: #14 mono canvas; 2-ply strands. Two and three-quarter strands (33 inches long) will cover one square inch.

Uses: Narrow strips; edging; elegant and decorative effects.

Remarks: Don't pull the fourth straight stitch tight before you place the needle into hole number 9.

Variations: 1) Thread a different color yarn through the row of horizontal stitches (without going through the canvas).

2) Make the small stitches in between a second color.

3) Enlarge the entire stitch.

4) Lay the stitches into each other by beginning the second stitch at hole number 9 and dropping it by half.

actual size

Sheaf stitch

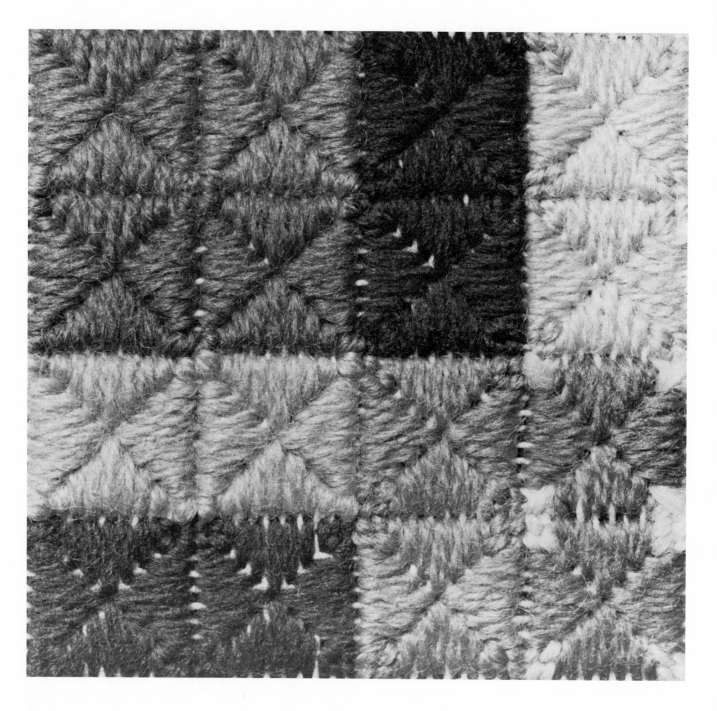

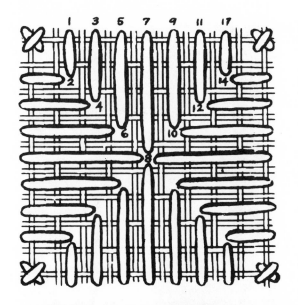

Triangle stitch

Materials: #14 mono canvas; 3-ply strands. One strand (33 inches long) will make one triangle.

Uses: Borders; special effects.

Remarks: This stitch cannot be divided, except diagonally into individual triangles. Be sure you have enough room for a complete stitch if making an area of triangle stitches. There will be a small space between the cross stitch and the first long stitch, but this will disappear in the blocking process.

Variation: Variety is obtained by use of color; two triangles may be done in one color and the other two in a second color, for example.

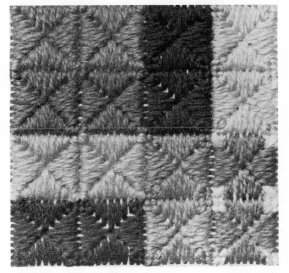

actual size

Triangle stitch

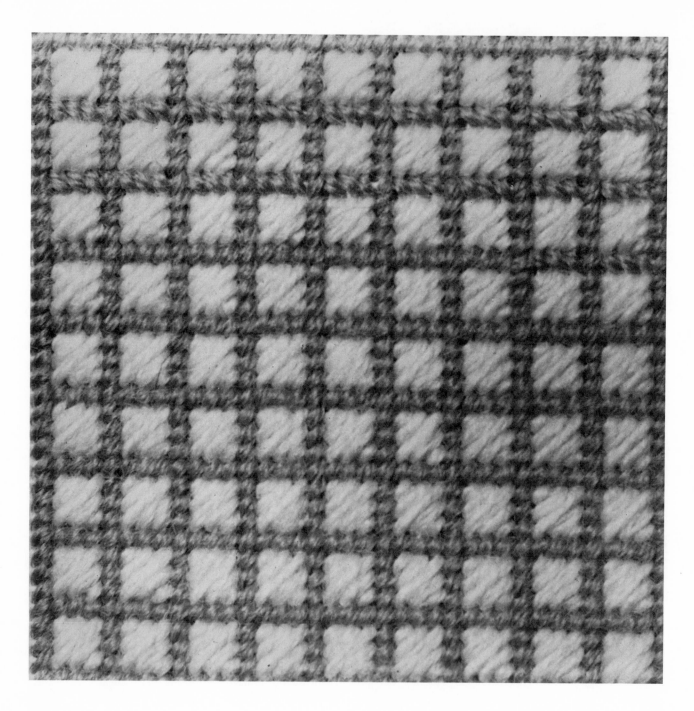

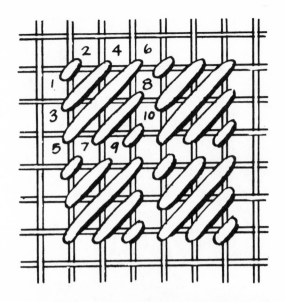

Scotch stitch

Materials: #14 mono canvas; 2-ply strands. Three strands (33 inches long) will cover one square inch.

Uses: Small patterns; background; for design, many uses.

Remarks: This is a versatile stitch with a thousand variations.

Variations:
1) Enclose each Scotch group in Half-Cross stitches.
2) Separate Scotch with equal amount of Half-Cross stitches (this produces a Checquer stitch).
3) Turn alternate Scotch stitches so that four combine into a large square, and put a cross or French knot in the center.
4) Weave a thread through a finished Scotch.

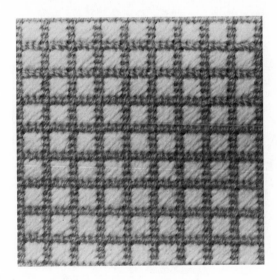

actual size

Scotch stitch

48

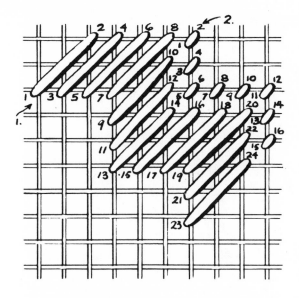

Jacquard stitch

Jacquard (or Byzantine) stitch

Materials: #14 mono canvas; 2-ply strands. Three and a third strands (33 inches long) will cover one square inch.

Uses: Large areas; background; special effects, such as stairsteps.

Remarks: Think of stairs and risers. Don't count the sharing stitch twice when counting. This stitch distorts the canvas somewhat.

Important: Always begin a new row with a full stitch and go back and fill in partials later.

Variations: This stitch is called the Byzantine stitch when no Half-Cross stitch separates it. Vary by use of color.

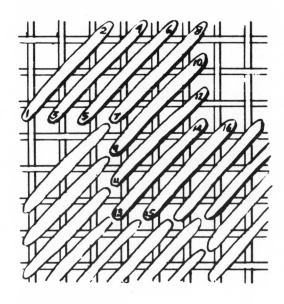

Byzantine stitch

actual size

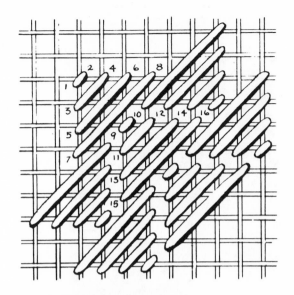

Milanese stitch

Materials: #14 mono canvas; 2-ply strands. Two and three-quarter strands (33 inches long) will cover one square inch.

Uses: Wavy effect, as in water; backgrounds; large areas.

Remarks: This stitch is lovely in one color or in two or more colors. Count carefully; the edges of the longest stitch will lie on a diagonal row of holes. This stitch distorts the canvas somewhat.

actual size

Milanese stitch

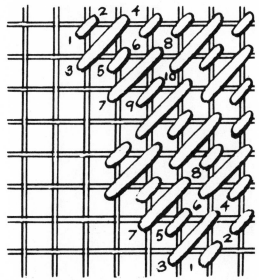

Diagonal Mosaic stitch

Materials: #14 mono canvas; 2-ply strands. Three strands (33 inches long) will cover one square inch.

Uses: Backgrounds; small areas; pattern effects.

Remarks: This stitch distorts canvas considerably but works around designs easily. If the large stitches only are worked in one row, and the smaller stitches filled in next, the distortion is diminished.

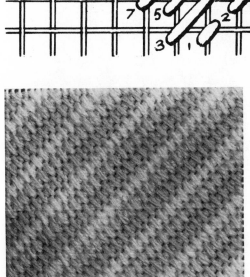

actual size

Diagonal Mosaic

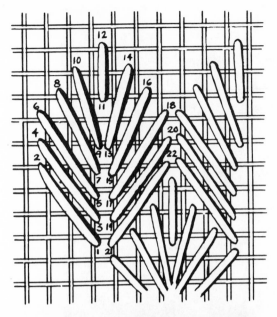

Leaf stitch

Materials: #14 mono canvas; 2-ply strands. Two strands (33 inches long) will cover one square inch.

Uses: Pattern; can be used separately as design motif; lovely in one color or for shadow effects.

Remarks: Count carefully, especially the empty hole between 9 and 11. The stitch is best worked diagonally, beginning second stitch on holes 6 or 18. Note that stitch number 2 is one hole above number 12 of the previous leaf.

Variations: Add or subtract length; use tips only; lay a stem up three holes.

actual size

Leaf stitch

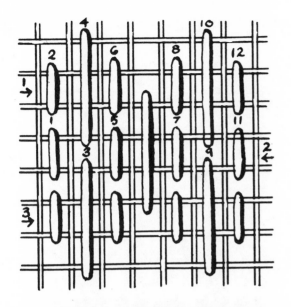

Hungarian stitch

Materials: #14 mono canvas; 3-ply strands. Two strands (33 inches long) will cover one square inch.

Uses: Backgrounds; to produce pattern effects — a versatile stitch.

Remarks: Work the stitches in the same direction — top to bottom or bottom to top. This stitch can be done in one color or in multiple colors; larger pattern can be worked out if two colors are used.

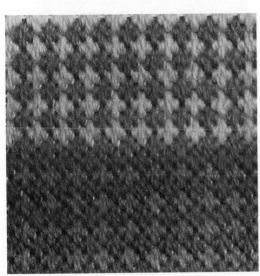

actual size

Hungarian stitch

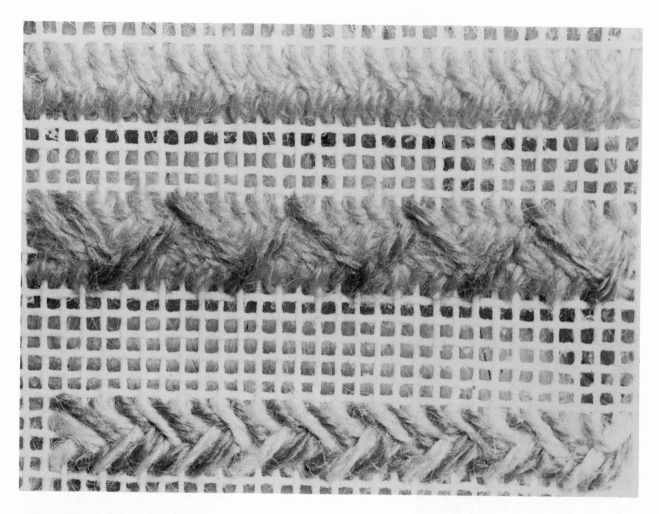

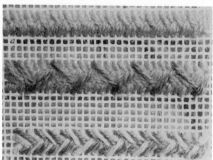

actual size

Herringbone Stitch (top) and variations:
Bazar (middle) and Woven band (bottom)

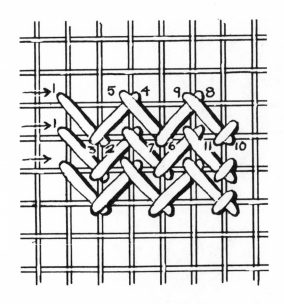

Herringbone stitch

Materials: #14 mono canvas; single-ply strands. Four and a half strands (33 inches long) will cover one square inch.

Uses: Narrow strips; border; larger pattern stitches.

Remarks: This stitch can be made as tall or short as desired. It is hard to see on small canvas. Always work left to right.

Variations: 1) Two-color.
2) Bazar stitch (taken from 1869 sampler).
3) Woven band.
4) "Herringbone-gone-wrong"; in this variation, one row is worked left to right and the next right to left.

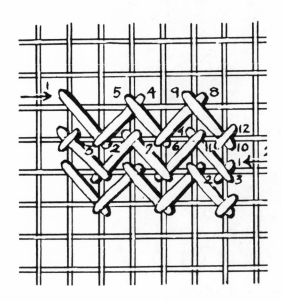

Herringbone stitch (top) and "Herringbone-gone-wrong"

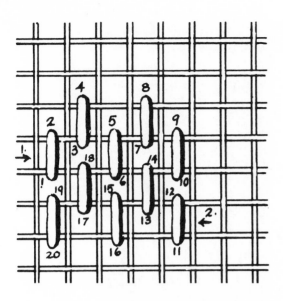

Brick stitch, variation 1; each stitch is worked in sequence.

Brick stitch

Materials: #14 mono canvas; 3-ply strands. One and three-quarter to two strands (33 inches long) will cover one square inch.

Uses: Background; to fill large or small areas; special effects. Fits with Bargello especially well.

Remarks: There are two ways of working this stitch. Variation 1 is adequate for most work. Variation 2 gives a firmer backing and therefore is a stronger-wearing stitch.

Brick stitch, variation 2; every other stitch is worked in one row, then the next row is worked in between.

actual size

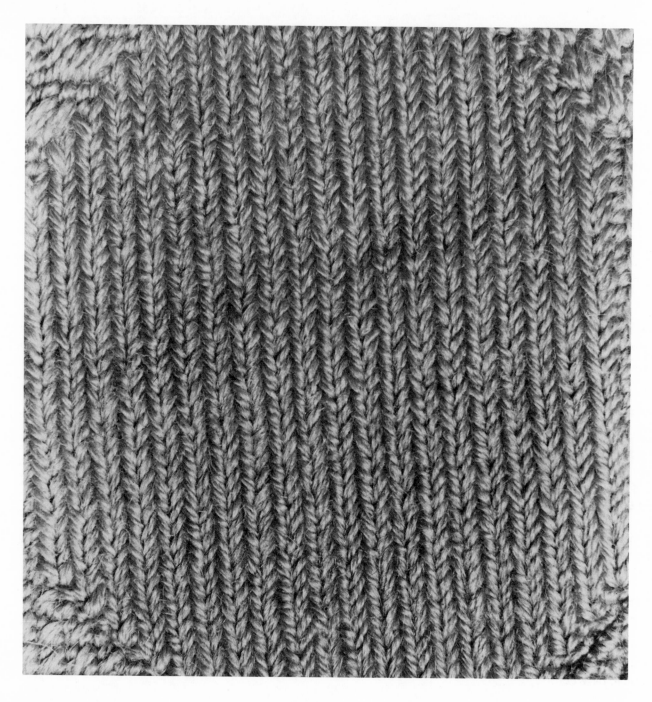

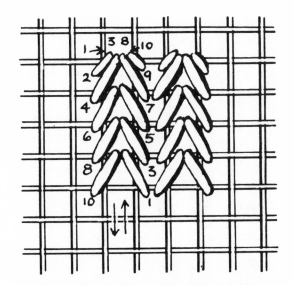

Kalem (or Knitting) stitch

Materials: #14 mono canvas; 2-ply strands. Four and a half strands will cover one square inch.

Uses: Stripes or braids; for separating larger areas.

Remarks: This stitch is called Kalem when worked vertically and Knitting when worked horizontally. It resembles a finely knit sweater. It boasts excellent wearability and is ideal for rugs. Patterns can be achieved by varying colors.

actual size

Kalem stitch

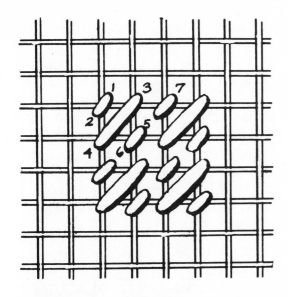

Mosaic stitch

Materials: #14 mono canvas; 2-ply strands. Two and three-quarter strands (33 inches long) will cover one square inch.

Uses: Small patterns, background.

Remarks: This is actually a smaller version of the Scotch stitch. It is a petite and dainty stitch that is best worked from right to left in an area. Do not work too tightly.

Variations: By color choice.

actual size

Mosaic stitch

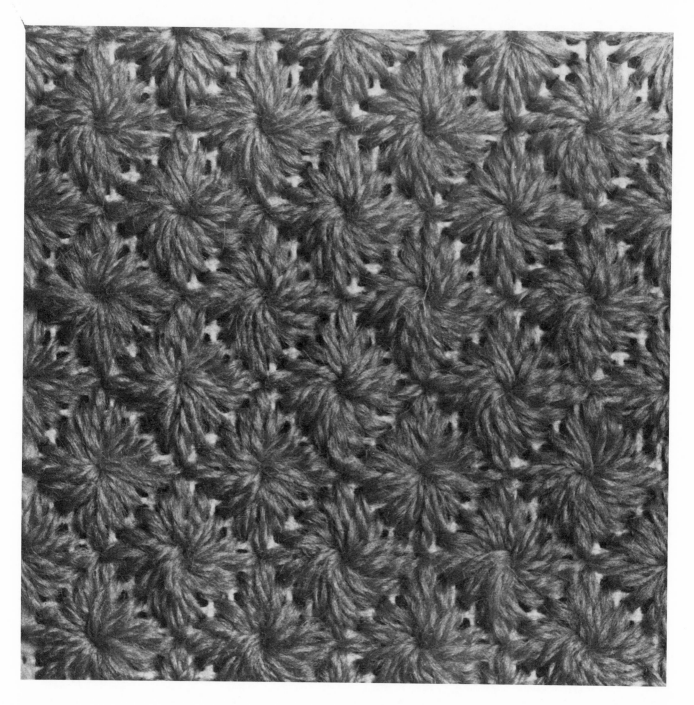

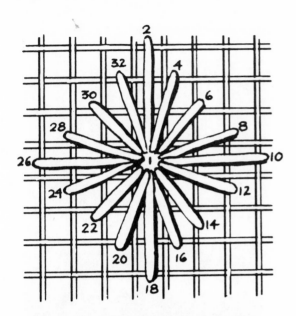

Diamond Eyelet stitch

Materials: #14 mono canvas; 2-ply strands. Four strands (33 inches long) will cover one square inch.

Uses: For accents.

Remarks: Always come forward (toward you) in an empty hole, back (away from you) through the center hole. Enlarging the center hole with the needle results in a dainty, open appearance. Since canvas may show around edges, back stitch may be used to surround eyelets.

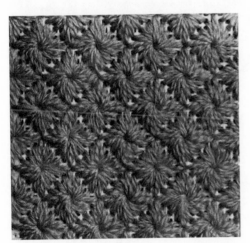

actual size

Diamond Eyelet stitch

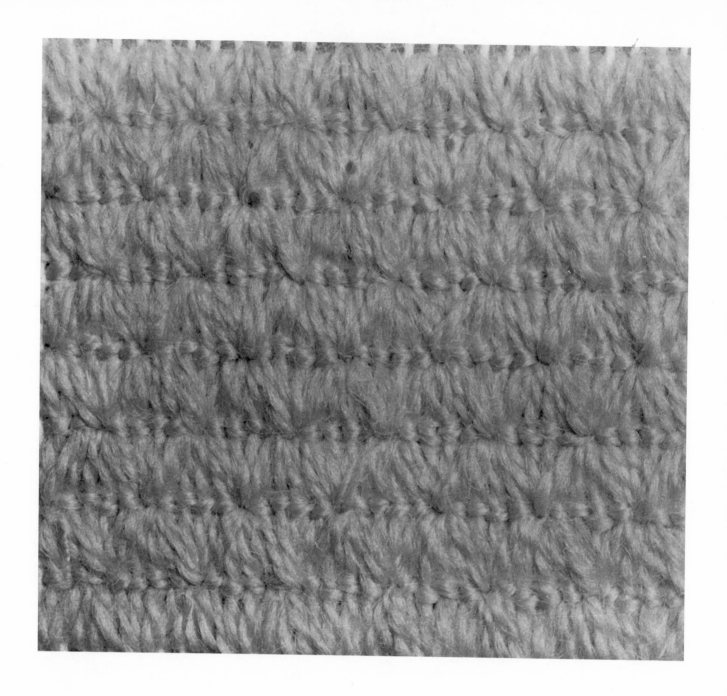

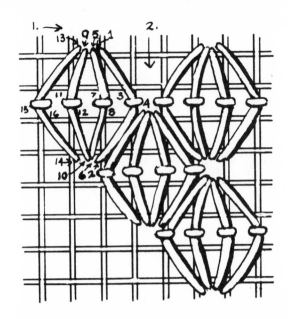

Rococo stitch

Materials: #14 mono canvas; single ply strands. Four strands (33 inches long) will cover one square inch.

Uses: Background; diagonal stripes; effect of roughness.

Remarks: Appearance of this stitch resembles rough tree bark. It is best worked in diagonal rows, although it can be worked horizontally.

Colonial Variation (also called Queen's stitch): With stiletto, enlarge the four extreme holes (4, 16, top, and bottom), pulling each stitch tightly. This variation makes a lacy look of the sort used widely in gentlemen's pocketbooks in Colonial America.

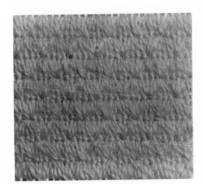

actual size

Rococo stitch

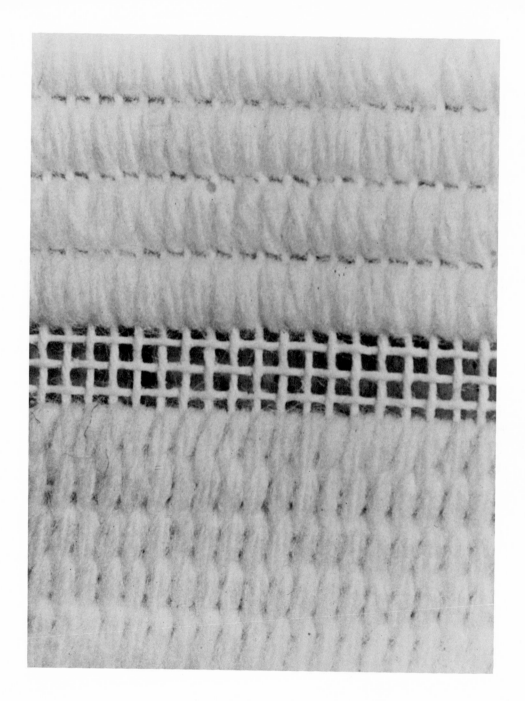

actual size

Gobelin stitch (top)
and encroaching
variation (lower)

Gobelin stitch

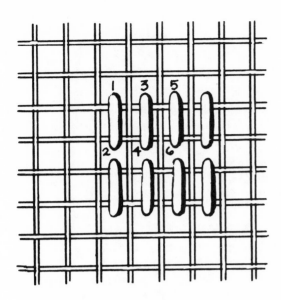

Gobelin stitch

Materials: #14 mono canvas; 3-ply strands. Four strands (33 inches long) will cover one square inch.

Uses: Backgrounds; pattern areas; shading. This is a versatile stitch. Its very smooth texture makes it good for shading.

Remarks: The Gobelin stitch is said to have been Martha Washington's favorite. Keep your yarn full and smooth; don't let it twist. The stitch is best worked on a frame.

Variations: 1) Slanted — slant to right one hole.

2) Encroaching — work second row into first row, taking care not to split yarn of first row. This variation is usually worked with a slanted Gobelin stitch.

3) Split — work second row into first, splitting each stitch. This is an excellent stitch for shading.

4) Oblique — the stitch is laid on its side rather than vertically.

5) Plaited — this version has a rough, woven look; keep your wool fat.

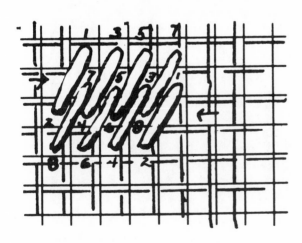

Gobelin stitch, encroaching variation

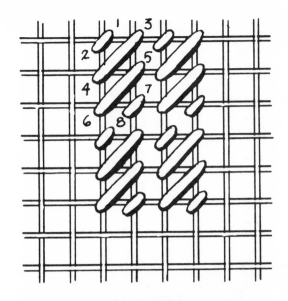

Cashmere stitch

Materials: #14 mono canvas; 2-ply strands. One and a half strands (33 inches long) will cover one square inch.

Uses: Background; pattern areas.

Remarks: This dainty and petite stitch is essentially the same as the Mosaic stitch, of which it is an enlarged version. It is lovely when separated and surrounded by Tent stitch.

actual size

Cashmere stitch

74

Turkey stitch

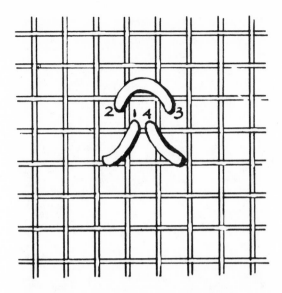

Materials: #14 mono canvas; 3 or more ply strands. Eight strands (33 inches long) will cover one square inch.

Uses: Special effects; rugs.

Remarks: This is also known as the Ghiordes knot. It is excellent for use in pile rugs or in furry areas of projects. Leave the ends of the yarn on the front of the project rather than working them into the back in the normal manner; a ruler or tongue depressor can be used to even the strands. Cut each row as worked, or don't cut the yarn at all, which will produce loops.

actual size

Turkey stitch

Hungarian-Point Bargello stitch

Bargello stitch

Materials: #14 mono canvas; 3-ply strands. Coverage varies with patterns.

Perhaps the most stunning of the needlepoint stitches is Bargello (pronounced bar-jéllo). It is a generic term, covering both Florentine and Hungarian-Point methods.

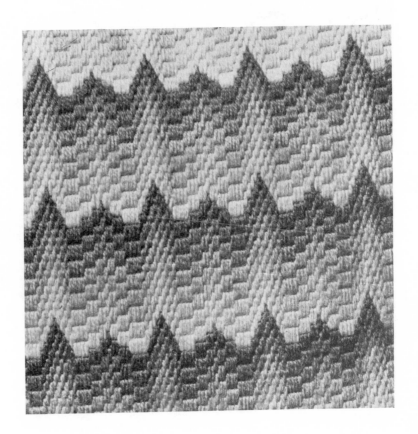

Florentine-style Bargello stitch

78

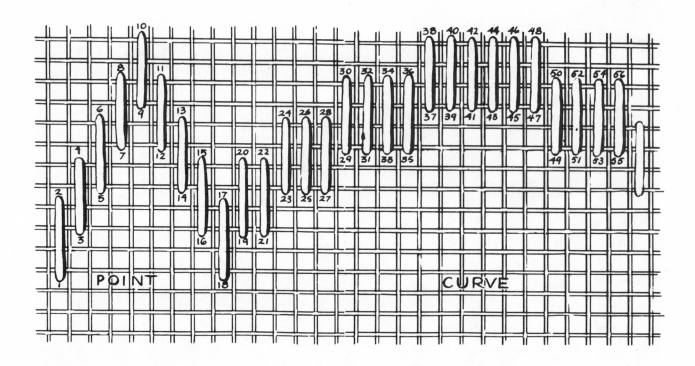

POINT CURVE

Florentine-style Bargello stitch

Both methods consist of vertical stitches which move with precise and numerical rhythm up and down to form an undulating pattern. The choice of color will make each project different, even though the same basic pattern may have been used.

When working the Florentine-style Bargello stitch, each vertical stitch covers exactly the same number of holes. This will mean that once the first row of Florentine is worked, the only consideration involved is change of color; each row is exactly like the first.

Some thought can be given, however, to whether you want the movement in sharp points or smoother half-circles. Moving after each stitch results in points. By adding stitches laid on the same horizontal plane, the points can be padded out into half-circles. A combination of the two is often desirable.

Hungarian-Point Bargello consists of stitches of varying lengths. Since each stitch is of a different size, each row fits into the row above in puzzle fashion until the beginning row is met again.

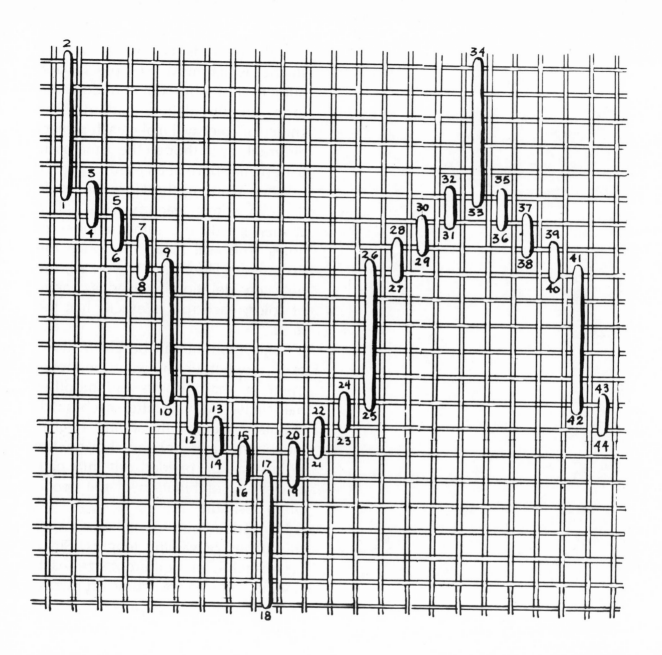

Hungarian-Point Bargello stitch

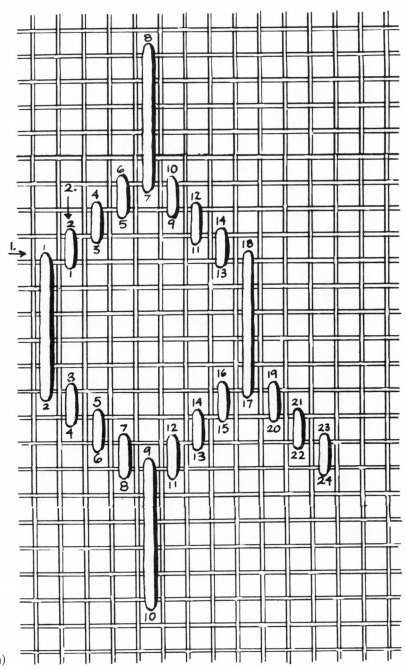

Hungarian-Point Bargello stitch (variation)

84

Traditionally, Bargello was worked in five shades of one color family. Today, many colors are typically combined to complement modern decor. The combination of colors is the "icing" of the Bargello stitch. Hold the skeins in your hand to get an idea of complementary combinations and to determine the order of use of the multiple colors.

By dividing your canvas corner to corner and forming a large X, a kaleidoscope of colors results — called Four-Way Bargello. Each triangle is the chosen basic pattern, but care is taken that they meet at the corners to form a box. In working this pattern, begin at the center — after marking the canvas to insure true diagonals — and work toward the outside. Each stitch abutting the slope of the diagonal will, obviously, be a different length.

These, then, are some basic, versatile, and useful stitches — not all there are, by any means, for there are literally hundreds of variations. Indeed, more stitches seem to be invented almost monthly.

Needlepoint is one art form in which you can't make a mistake; all you do is invent a new stitch.

Chapter 5

Blocking

When your project is finished, it's time to block it. Every project should be blocked whether it appears to need blocking or not. The procedure fluffs the wool and makes each strand rounder and smoother, improving the appearance of the finished piece. Some stitches, moreover, tend to warp the canvas, and blocking will restore the project to the desired shape.

The idea behind blocking is to wet the wool but to leave the canvas as dry as possible. There are several ways of achieving this, depending on how badly out of shape your stitches have pulled the canvas and how dirty the project may have become as you worked it.

If the piece is neither out of shape nor dirty, just pinning it to an ironing board and holding a steam iron over it may be sufficient blocking. Be sure not to touch the needlepoint with the iron, however! After steaming, leave the project untouched until it is perfectly dry, then unpin it and you're ready to go.

If the project is just a little out of shape, try rolling

it in wet (damp, not soggy-wet) bath towels. Leave the whole thing rolled up for several hours or overnight; the yarn will absorb the dampness.

Projects that are severely warped can be run under tepid water. Keep the project in continual motion while the water runs over it (the water temperature should be lukewarm). The natural oil in the wool will keep the canvas from becoming excessively wet in this process, but the wool itself will absorb enough water to be sufficiently wet for blocking.

If the project is quite dirty, wash it gently in Woolite or a similar product. Use water that is cool to tepid. Lay the piece in the wash water for three minutes, and then rinse under running water. Handle the project very gently, because canvas is vulnerable to damage when it's wet. If the sizing is completely washed off, there's little left but "noodles." To remove the excess water, roll the washed project in a dry towel.

While the project is wet, pin it to a blocking board. Use a bulletin board, a cork board, a ceiling tile, or any clean board that will accept pins easily without crumbling. Needless to say, the board must be larger than your project.

When you're ready to block, draw the exact finished dimensions of your project on a clean piece of paper and pin the paper to the board. This will provide a guide during the pinning and blocking so you get the corners square and the edges straight.

Be sure to use blocking pins that are rustproof. T-pins are most commonly used. Stainless steel thumbtacks are also good; they are available at business supply stores. You'll need about 70 pins for a project of normal size.

When the board is ready and the project has been dampened, place it face-up on the board, smooth it as much as possible, and then begin pinning at the middle of the top edge of the project; work toward each corner, gently stretching and straightening as you go.

When the top is completely pinned, move to the bottom edge; pull the project gently but firmly until the bottom edge coincides with the bottom line on your guide drawing. Start again in the middle of the bottom edge and work toward each corner.

Repeat the process on the two sides, always working from the middle of an edge outward to the corners. By the time you get to the last side, some good, strong pulling may be necessary. While it is damp, the piece can be stretched to any reasonable size. It will shrink slightly as it dries, pulling the work taut.

When the pinning is done, lay the blocking board flat and let it dry. If you prop the board so that it stands upright or on a slant, the water will seep to the lower portion of the project and may cause a water stain.

Be sure the project is perfectly dry before you remove it from the board. Depending on the method used in dampening the piece — and the humidity — this will take anywhere from twenty-four hours to a week. Sometimes it's hard to keep from unpinning the project prematurely, but resist the urge; if you unpin too soon, you may have to reblock.

Chapter 6

Projects and Finishing

Your project is now designed, worked, and blocked. What do you do next? You can put it in a drawer and go on to something else, but why deny your family and friends the joy of seeing the fruits of your work? This chapter will provide some tips on common finishing procedures for numerous projects available to needlepoint.

Two general rules for all projects are to Scotchguard them after blocking, and to stitch along the outside edge of the work on the sewing machine before beginning assembly.

Pillows

Finishing a pillow can cost a considerable sum if you have professionals do it, but it's inexpensive and quite easy to do at home for anyone who sews.

Backing materials are usually rich, in keeping with the appearance of the project. Velvet, crushed velvet, ribbed and non-ribbed corduroy, plain and watered taffeta, upholstery material, and polyester double knit are the more common backings. The material shouldn't be too thick and bulky, because the needlepoint itself is quite heavy and some sewing machines balk at too much thickness. Polyester double knit is ideal because of its stretch qualities and the heaviness of the material, but those very qualities call for care in handling so that it doesn't stretch while being sewn.

To begin with, you'll have to decide which of the two types of pillows you want to create: knife edge or box edge. On the knife-edge style, the front (your project) and the backing are joined directly. The box-edge pillow will have a third piece of material separating the front from the back. Knife-edge pillows are easier to make, but some of the effect of the border design is inevitably lost due to the dome shape of the pillow.

Whether you choose a knife edge or a box edge, you may want to finish the pillow with cording or twisted yarn. Or you may prefer to leave the edges plain and put tassels on the corners.

Cording can be bought already covered or plain, to be covered by you with the backing material. When covering your own (usually the better idea), cut a strip of material three inches wide (don't worry about cutting on the diagonal of the material, since it will be sewn on straight seams), fold the material over the cord evenly, and stitch as closely as possible, using the zipper foot of the machine.

Attach cording to the pillow top before putting the pillow together. Begin at the bottom edge and lay

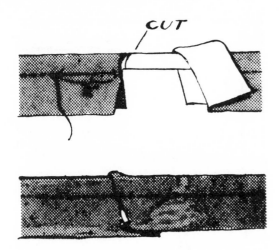

CUT

Cording corner

the cording on the front of the blocked pillow with the cording facing toward the center of the work and the raw edge toward the outside. Leaving about the first two inches unsewn, begin stitching in the middle of the bottom edge and work toward the first corner. At that point, with the needle down through the layers, raise the foot of the machine and carefully snip the selvage edges of the cording as far as the stitching; this gives you a neat, square corner. Turn the pillow and stitch on around to the starting point, clipping each corner in turn.

When you're about two inches from the place where you started, stop again, leaving the needle down to anchor the project. Raise the foot and measure the cording to the starting point. Cut off any excess, leaving a one and one-half inch overlap of material.

Now, opening the end piece, cut the cord at the spot that allows the two ends of the cord just to meet. Layer the extra material over the beginning piece of unsewn cording, turning in the end slightly, and stitch down the doubled material. The resulting joint will be almost invisible.

When the cording has been sewn to the top panel of the pillow (or if there is no cording), you are ready to make a knife-edge pillow as follows:

Lay the backing piece against the front so that the "outside" faces of the panels face each other; in other words, so the pillow is inside out. Starting at the bottom edge, with the needlepoint side up and about an inch and a half or two inches from the left corner, begin to stitch around the pillow following the rows of stitches separating the design from the extra three rows. When you've again reached the bottom of the pillow, stitch two inches into the bottom and stop. Trim the excess material and canvas to one-half inch, trimming closer at the corners. Turn the pillow right side out and insert the pillow form. Complete the stitching by hand.

Box-edge pillows require an extra step. The boxing strip is first sewn to the needlepoint all the way around, and then the backing piece is sewn to the boxing strip. The secret to making a good box-edge pillow is always to mark both edges of the boxing strip at each corner at one time. This will help you put the corner of the backing material at precisely the same point of the boxing strip as the corner of the front of the pillow, and thus will keep the boxing smooth. The alternative is an out-of-kilter and probably lumpy pillow.

An opening will have to be left between the boxing strip and the backing piece for the insertion of the pillow form. Cording, when it is used at all, is usually attached to both back and front edges of the boxing strip.

The pillow "form" is a shaped slab of polyester which goes inside the pillow. Forms can be purchased in needlepoint shops or department stores, and some variety stores also carry them. They provide a solid filling and give you a rather firm pillow. Some allow for dry-cleaning.

For softer pillows, you may prefer to use loose foam. This is powdery and tends to fly about as you pour it, so it's best to make a muslin lining a little

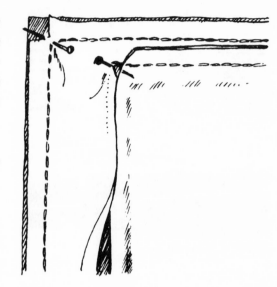

The secret of a good box-edge pillow is to mark both edges of the boxing strip at each corner at the same time.

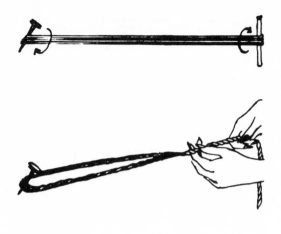

Reverse twist

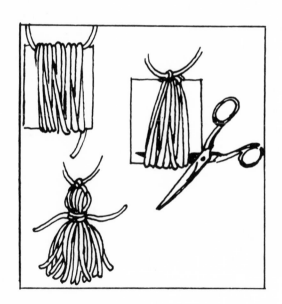

Tassel

larger than the pillow and put the foam in the lining before inserting the foam-filled liner in the pillow.

Sheet foam can be purchased in sheets at upholstery shops; it is easy to cut with an electric knife. When you cut a pillow form out of sheet foam, trim it slightly larger than the finished pillow; this provides a rounded or humped effect.

Other materials can be used as pillow stuffing, including nylon hose and dry-cleaners' plastic bags. It takes an ample supply of either to stuff a normal size pillow.

If you don't wish to use cording, a twist of yarn will make an attractive finished edge. Using two or three strands of yarn three times longer than the total perimeter of the pillow, fasten one end of the yarn securely to a nail or doorknob and then twist counterclockwise until the twist becomes so tight it begins to kink. Holding the middle in one hand, join the two ends and gently twist clockwise. Stitch this to the edge of the finished pillow with invisible thread.

Tassels make a lovely finishing touch for a pillow. Cut a cardboard pattern whose width equals the length of the desired tassel. Wrap yarn around the pattern until it's fairly thick. Then run a piece of yarn under the wrapped yarn at one edge, and tie this wound yarn together. Cut the yarn at the other edge of the cardboard and tie another piece of yarn about an inch down from the top, gathering all the yarn together into a tassel which can be attached to the pillow by the yarn at the top.

Drapery and upholstery fringe can also be sewn

on the pillow with invisible thread. Two rows of Turkey stitch worked around the edge before the pillow is sewn together make a handsome edging; this procedure requires about an ounce of yarn.

Eyeglass Cases

Eyeglass cases are made so rapidly that they are perfect gift items. Measure the width, length, and depth of the glasses, and add one-half inch in width and one inch in depth. The canvas can be cut so that the back and front are connected at the sides, thus forming a square, or at the bottom edge, thus forming a very long rectangle. Cut three extra mesh on each side. Carefully turn the extra mesh so that the holes match. Work the entire case, working over the doubled canvas for the outside borders.

When any project requires a firm edge, or has two sections of canvas to be sewn together (such as eyeglass cases, box edges, and typewriter covers), the Binding stitch offers a beautiful pattern combined with necessary strength. Used to stitch around the edges of rugs, it offers a strong edging that is fairly impervious to wear. For the eyeglass case, this stitch will be put first across the top of the case to bind the opening; then the case will be folded and the edges will be bound together by the stitch. A soft lining is made separately and inserted into the finished case and blind-stitched to the top of the opening.

The Binding stitch requires fewer ply than most,

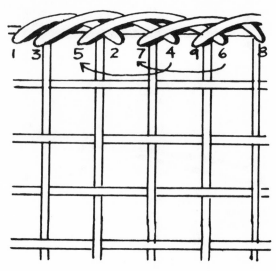

Binding stitch; always drawing the needle from back to front (toward you), make figure eights working left to right and advancing one hole with each stitch.

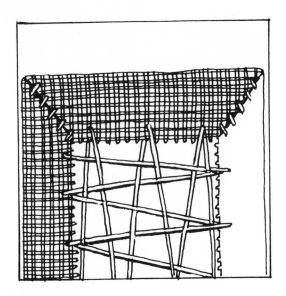

Sewn back

since the same areas are covered more than once. For all projects except rugs, one ply should be ample.

The work will always progress from left to right; the beginning end of the yarn should be laid on top and the stitches worked over it. Shorter stitches are needed at the beginning and end of a row to cover, but the rhythm after the first stitch will be three forward and two back. Since the needle is always brought from the back toward the worker, this will form a figure eight.

Ingenuity is required if you want to turn a corner with this stitch. Turning corners always requires smaller stitches. I also recommend painting the canvas at the corner to match the thread.

Pictures

Pictures do not require the three rows of extra stitches around the outside edge of the project as do some of the other finished pieces. They are worked to the exact size desired and the excess canvas is then turned back over a piece of cardboard which serves as a stiffener. Glue the excess canvas to the cardboard, or lace the canvas together — top to bottom and side to side — in order to hold the piece in place. Miter the corners by turning down the point, leaving a diagonal line across the top, and then folding each side down to square the corner; stitch the corner "ears" together. Now fit the picture into the

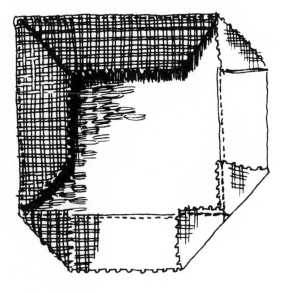

Miter corner

frame and cover the back with brown paper. If you sponge the paper slightly damp, it will pull taut when it dries.

The better practice is not to put the needlepoint under glass. Glass takes away all of the handwork look and dulls the impression. Spraying the finished work with Scotchguard, then dusting frequently, is all that is needed to keep a project clean.

However, there are times when you'll want to use glass. If so, spend the small additional amount to buy nonglare glass, which causes less distortion. There should be at least one-half to three-fourths of an inch of air between the needlepoint and the glass. This can be provided by using a shadow box frame or by wedging cardboard between the frame and the needlepoint where it won't show. This space is needed to keep the needlepoint from being mashed by the glass and also to retard the danger of mildew.

Picture Frames and Mirror Frames

Needlepoint adds greatly to a picture when used as a matting frame. If you undertake this kind of project, don't cut out the blank center of the canvas (where the picture will go) until the entire project is finished and blocked. When you do remove the center, leave a half inch of canvas all around the inside perimeter of the matting. Cut diagonally to the corners to allow for folding back. Finally, place the project on the precut stiffener and secure the needlework as you would for a needlepoint picture (above), using either glue or lacing.

Another interesting use of needlepoint is to create an edge or "frame" for a mirror. This can be done with or without a cardboard stiffener. If you don't use a stiffener, work the canvas doubled and use the Binding stitch around the inside edge. It is wise to line this project so that the back does not reflect in the mirror and spoil the image. To attach the needlepoint frame to the mirror, use glue.

Pockets, Vests, Belts, and Clothing

Clothing decoration in general is best done on nylon canvas since it is lightweight and soft. It wears well and can even be washed.

Pockets are an easy and attractive way of displaying your handiwork. They are made by turning the edges back and working both layers of canvas with the Binding stitch to complete the pocket. Line the pocket with a soft material before blind-stitching it to your jacket or other article of apparel. If desired, it can be outlined with braid after being attached to the jacket. Stitch the braid with invisible thread.

Vests and cummerbunds are investments in beauty. Because needlepoint can be heavy, you may want to use floss or silk instead of wool. You'll certainly want to use nylon canvas. It is wise to work only the front rather than the entire piece. Any good pattern can be used when making a vest, but one with no darts — or very few — is best. If there are darts, do not work them in needlepoint, but sew them together and cut them after all is finished and blocked.

Vests and cummerbunds should be lined. Satin, taffeta, a lightweight polyester, or even cotton would be suitable as long as it complements the needlepoint. If more stiffness is needed, iron-on Pellon (obtainable at any fabric department) offers stiffness without weight.

Belts are especially attractive. They can be made in any width desired, and in any length. Buckles are usually large, of the clasp variety rather than the type using tongues and holes. Make the belt several inches longer than necessary and overlap one end. Cut the canvas an inch longer and an inch wider than the finished length and width of the belt. Turn one-half inch in, doubling the canvas, on all four sides. Work the belt, working over the doubled canvas, and then put the Binding stitch on the top and the bottom (or the long sides). Fold the ends over the buckle, stitch with invisible thread, and you have a belt.

Incidentally, belts are best lined, and grosgrain ribbon is ideal for this purpose.

Rugs

Rugs are a large undertaking and are quite attractive when finished. If the proper stitches are used —

stitches with good backing and relatively short front threads — the rug will be as durable and cleanable as any broadloom, and need not be treated as a fragile item.

There are two methods of working a rug:

In the English method you turn back about 12 inches on the cut end of the canvas before beginning work; the Binding stitch is worked over the turn and down both sides for a way, then work is begun over doubled canvas on the pattern. Thought must be given at the other end to allow for the foldback before the end of the pattern is reached.

The Binding stitch gives a firm, smooth edge that is extremely hardwearing under foot. It is also attractive. In this method there is no lining cloth. Thus dirt from shoes falls through to the floor where it can be swept up easily with the vacuum cleaner.

With the American method you turn the edges under after the canvas has been worked completely, using a binding tape. Then a muslin or monk's cloth is used to line the entire rug. Dirt is held in this lining and, unless removed, will wear the underneath side of the yarn.

On all rugs, a heavy coating of rabbit-skin glue (see Chapter 7) is a necessity. Not only will it hold the blocked shape, it will also give body and firmness to the rug.

For ease, rugs can be worked in small sections and put together later. Overlapping canvas is the firmest and easiest of connections. In this method, a section of the design is left unworked on the edges of each section. These sections are then overlapped on the unworked edges, and the design is finished by working over the doubled canvas.

Another connection can be made by working both sections fully, tacking the excess (unworked) canvas to the back, placing the pieces right sides together, and whipping them down. Care must be taken to see that the mesh are perfectly aligned.

In making a rug, a frame is extremely useful. Blocking a large piece of canvas is strenuous, and if the canvas is quite out of shape it may be impossible to straighten. Frames keep the work even so that blocking is needed only to fluff the wool.

Rugs may be made with a short pile or a long pile, as well as with flat stitches. When Oriental rugs are woven, the weaver ties a row of Ghiordes knots (Turkey stitch), weaves several rows of weft, and then ties another row of knots. Needlepoint canvas supplies the rows of weft. Thus pile rugs greatly resemble Oriental rugs.

The knots will accommodate any length of yarn pile. Long pile — two inches or more — is known as Rya. Short pile can be made to resemble Oriental or broadloom or any other pile rug. Cutting the pile into varying lengths offers a modern choice which is quite attractive.

Flat stitches offer a variety of texture and appearance. Basketweave is probably the strongest and most versatile. Here the emphasis will be on color and design, rather than on texture.

Other stitches suitable for rugs are:

Rice stitch (exceptionally long wearing and sturdy;
 sometimes known as the rug stitch)

Long-armed Cross stitch (another long-wearing stitch)
Cross stitch
Kalem or Knitting stitch
Brick stitch
Rococo stitch
Hungarian stitch
French stitch

The size of mesh chosen will determine the textural stitch. All of them will supply good design and texture. If a small mesh is used, such as #14 or #16, a Bargello stitch or the Leaf stitch will also make long-wearing rugs.

Canvases of #3 and #5 mesh are thought of as rug canvas. These take rug yarn or three to four full strands of Persian yarn to cover. This size is best for pile rugs. However, there is not too much room for small designs, such as cabbage roses and the like. Modern geometric patterns work well.

Smaller size canvas — #10 to #14 — works up more slowly but offers a larger range of design and stitches.

Before beginning a rug, determine where it will be placed; this will indicate the amount of wear it will receive and the finished size of the project. Then choose the design. Once these details are known, the size canvas to be worked and the stitches to be used can be determined, and the colors chosen to suit the area.

Rugs should be made of wool for long wear. Cotton and the acrylics do not have the durability or resistance of wool.

Chapter 7
Problems and Tips

Everyone who tries a hand at needlework — or anything else worthwhile — will occasionally encounter problems. This chapter suggests ways to solve a few, as well as offering some miscellaneous tips to make your work more professional. If you encounter a problem not touched on here, don't panic. Give the obstacle your best creative thinking and you may be able to invent your own solution. If that doesn't work, call a friend who has had more experience in the art of needlepoint and see if your problem isn't one that's been encountered by others; chances are it is.

Cut canvas is probably the worst problem you'll run into while working on a project. It is easily corrected by placing under the cut a square of the same mesh canvas, but about an inch larger than the damaged section. Take care to line up the mesh evenly. Stitch through both pieces of canvas as if they were a single canvas after trimming away any ragged edges from the damaged canvas.

Sectioning canvas is a way to meet the problem of working with a very large project such as a rug. It consists of cutting the project into smaller and more workable pieces, then reassembling the whole project. In the reassembling process, you'll be working through two layers of overlapping canvas which have previously been completed except for the edges at which they'll be joined. Make the joint by overlapping or layering at least six inches of canvas. As you work the overlapped section, you will automatically create a seam which is all but invisible. The canvases should be basted together with sewing thread before working the layered section, so that the mesh will remain even and not slip out of line. When working the sections originally, remember to leave the portion of the design unworked that will go over the seam.

Dirty threads can cause you headaches. Some shades of yarn tend to pick up dirt while they're being worked. Another cause of dirty threads is a canvas marking which rubs off on yarn, leaving a streaked row. About the only real solution to dirty threads is to pick out the offending yarn and replace it with fresh. Needless to say, you should begin every needlepoint session with clean hands.

Thin threads occur occasionally because some dyes react with yarn in a way that leaves the yarn thinner than similar yarn in another color. The problem becomes one of coverage. To solve this difficulty, simply use more plies of the offending color. Green seems to be a particular culprit.

You should also pay attention to the length of the yarn you're working. Very long pieces of yarn tend to stretch, under the pulling and tension of stitches, in the direction of the end of the strand. Thus the stitches at the end of the yarn may be thinner than those at the beginning. The solution to this problem is to cut shorter strands.

Twisted threads are a problem with two easy solutions. No matter how carefully stitches are laid, thread tends to twist before the whole length has been worked. The canvas should be held up occasionally to let the thread dangle free, like a kinked telephone cord, until it straightens itself out. Leave the needle in the end to give weight and momentum to the unraveling strand. An alternative solution is to roll your needle counterclockwise between your fingers with each stitch. This counteracts the tendency toward clockwise turning of the yarn which occurs naturally as you turn your needle away from you and toward you. Keeping threads untwisted is essential to fine needlepoint.

Rough-appearing work can be caused by any of several things. One is scooping your thread instead of using two distinct motions to make each stitch. Uneven tension and twisted threads are another cause. Be sure to work all stitches in correct sequence to avoid a sloppy-looking finished project; for example, when laying two vertical stitches next to each other, begin both at either the top or the bottom — otherwise the yarn will tend to make the stitches fall apart from each other, creating a ridge.

Mismarked canvas is a correctable problem. Designs are best worked originally on paper which can be erased or thrown away, and then transferred to the canvas. Even so, you may mark the canvas incorrectly occasionally, causing confusion later as you work on the project. To remove an incorrect line, apply some white acrylic paint thinned to a consistency that will cover the offending marks but won't fill in the holes in the canvas. When the paint is dry, spray the painted area with clear acrylic spray to set it permanently. Then re-mark the correct design.

This is a good place to repeat a caution mentioned earlier in the book. Any time you have doubt about the waterproof quality of a marking pen, it's wise to spray the marks with clear acrylic spray. Discovering pen marks after the piece is worked will leave you with no recourse but tears . . . and ripping out sections of your work.

Rabbit-skin glue may be used as a sizing when a piece is so badly out of shape that blocking must be repeated often to hold the shape. This glue, available at most needlepoint stores, can also be used when you want a firm texture because of the kind of project you're doing — a purse, for example. The glue is a strong sizing which will hold a project in shape and give it backing. Rabbit-skin glue comes in powder form, to which water is added to make a medium-thick gruel. Brush it on with a clean paint brush and let it dry.

Accidents can happen to such items as chair seats and upholstery after your project is done. They can be fixed by removing the broken threads and replacing them. Since it may be hard to match wool colors exactly, place a few extra strands of each color in the design under a chair seat or in some inconspicuous portion of any upholstered project when you are making it up; then you'll have spare yarn in the right dye lot to make repairs with later. Just pick out the marred section, place new canvas under it if needed, and stitch the mend in. Should the canvas be damaged, mend as instructed for cut canvas (above).

Use light colors first when you have a mixture of light and dark yarns in a project. The hairs of the dark yarn tend to color the light yarn slightly if dark stitches are put down before light.

Ends of threads should always be kept on the back of the canvas and neatly trimmed. Clip each end as close as possible to the work after running it through the back of some stitches to lock it in place. Ends tend to work up toward the front of a project when you apply other colors in their vicinity.

Threading more than one needle may be a convenience when you're working a design that calls for very small sections of color. It's simply easier to thread the various colors and leave them in the project than to be constantly rethreading for tiny work areas. When not using a given color, bring the unused amount of that thread to the front of the project so it doesn't get caught while you work another color.

When working patterns with several small areas of a color, it is all right to carry the thread from one section to the next, so long as the long piece of yarn will be locked down later by the intervening stitches.

Changing the size of a pattern to make it fit your project is not difficult. You can either enlarge or scale down the pattern by using a different size of canvas mesh than the original design called for. You can figure the proportions by using an inverse-ratio method: a 15-inch square worked on a #5 canvas, for example, will become a 7½-inch square worked on a #10 canvas — or a 5-inch square worked on a #15 canvas. The larger the mesh size, the larger your project will be.

part

III

Principles of Design

Victorian-style sampler, incorporating family dreams and accomplishments. (Work of Audrey Thompson.)

Chapter 8

Design It Yourself

Although there are many lovely needlepoint kits on the market, inexpensive and costly, many practitioners of the art maintain that happiness is designing your own canvases. It's not nearly so difficult as you might think if you haven't tried it.

Choosing the colors that appeal to you, searching out and incorporating into a design your favorite symbols and interests, seeing your own ideas move from inside your head to the canvas — all this provides a sense of accomplishment that will add both aesthetic and financial value to a needlepoint project. Rare is the kit that can provide as much satisfaction as a self-designed piece.

But, you say, you're not an artist? You can't draw a straight line with a ruler? Don't let it worry you. You can learn all you need to know to create your own designs if you want to. And since the canvas is woven in straight lines, *that* problem is eliminated.

The first step in creating a design is to find an idea to work with. Ideas are all around you. All it takes is knowing where to look for them.

Family home, adapted by Mary Riedle

What are your family's favorite hobbies — flowers, birds, nature? What architectural style do you find appealing? What decorating period characterizes the room in which you will display your project — Colonial, modern, Chinese? Do you prefer abstract or naturalistic designs, geometric or expressionistic patterns, finely detailed or large, buoyant works of art? Your preferences will be reflected in your design creations — and will make them uniquely yours.

Books provide an endless supply of design ideas.

Adaptation of ancient Chinese statue for chair pillow placed next to statue (by Inda Katts)

If you have doubts about your artistic ability don't be afraid to copy pleasing elements from various books and put them together into a design you like. Bird-identification books, flower catalogues, herbals, quilt patterns, geometric designs, ancient mosaic tiles and modern tiles — these sources have been inspiring needleworkers for centuries. You might want to create a design that borrows from wallpaper or upholstery so your project will contribute special elegance to a room. China patterns can be adapted for needlepoint designs to be used on chairs, place mats, or wall hangings for the dining room. The pictures on the labels of fruit or vegetable cans can contribute charming designs for kitchen projects.

Do you have a collection of postcards from especially memorable vacation spots? Adapt your favorite to a needlepoint design. Try copying a favorite work of art, whether it's a painting or a sculpture, for a project design. Some children's games, like "Splatter Paint" or "Spirograph," can help you create enticing patterns. Trace your pre-schooler's drawing to capture it in wool and turn it into an heirloom; your child will share the joy and pride of having helped design your project. Look carefully at a small section of a fruit or vegetable and see if it doesn't suggest an abstract design. Or examine closely a small portion of a picture, of a piece of tree bark, or of a leaf — all can inspire abstract patterns. Remember when you were a child and you folded and cut paper patterns like snowflakes? Try it now, and see if the results suggest pattern ideas.

The key word in all this is "adaptation." If you

Adaptation of a design taken from a kitchen calendar-towel, by June Derda

Bicentennial fireplug design,
adapted by Vera Slack

copy exactly from a book, a postcard, or a picture, you'll get no more real satisfaction than if you work a needlepoint kit — and you may end up a great deal more frustrated. You will, when all is said and done, be using someone else's ideas. But you can "adapt" — choosing portions of a printed design or tracing the outline of an object from a book — without copying an entire idea. Put together your borrowings into something new and the end product will be truly yours.

When you do borrow from books, keep in mind that a lot of detail is not possible with needlepoint (unless you're doing petit point). It really isn't necessary, either. Borrow the essential identifying features and ignore the rest. Simplification is a good rule in designing needlepoint projects.

You may end up with a pattern that doesn't "fit" your project. You can, if you wish, take it to a photo shop or print shop and have the design enlarged or made smaller mechanically. Or you can change the size yourself through graphing. Here's how it's done.

To enlarge, trace the pattern first, then draw a grid of lines one-quarter inch apart over the drawing. Make another grid, with half-inch spaces, next to it. Copy the design square by square from the small to the large grid. The result will be your design twice as large as the original. Changing the ratio of the two grids lets you increase the pattern by any factor you choose.

To make a pattern smaller, reverse the process. Draw a half-inch grid on the tracing and a smaller

grid next to it, then transfer the pattern square by square. If each square isn't exactly perfect, don't worry too much. When it gets onto the canvas, small anomalies will not be noticeable.

Always work your design on paper until you're satisfied with the results. Only then should you transfer the design to canvas. The transfer can be accomplished in several ways.

The easiest way is simply to lay the design — overdrawn with dark, black ink — underneath the canvas. The pattern will show clearly through the holes of the canvas; if it doesn't, placing a light behind the pattern and the canvas will make the design more visible. An artist's table, which has a glass top and a light underneath, is a good way to secure the necessary light, or you can tape the pattern and canvas to a window and use sunlight to highlight the pattern. Now use your waterproof marking pen to trace the pattern onto the canvas.

Somewhat more complicated but ultimately a more satisfactory method is to copy the pattern onto graph paper the size of the canvas. Use graph paper whose squares equal one stitch on the canvas. With this method, you work with an unmarked canvas counting stitches from the graph-paper guide. Drawbacks of this method are the fact that you have to keep the paper always with you as you work the project, and the fact that it tends to be hard on the eyes — especially if you wear bifocals.

Under certain conditions, you may want to paint your canvas to match the colors of the yarn you're using. You can use either oil or acrylic paints after thinning them. Acrylics dry much faster than oil paints. It's wise to spray painted sections with clear acrylic spray after the paint is dry to fix the colors. Painting your canvas insures that you'll use the correct color yarn for the painted area, with the bonus that it avoids any tendency for the white canvas to show through thin stitches.

A technique commonly used since medieval times is to lay across the canvas a piece of the same color yarn you're using to stitch in that area. It is an alternative to painting the canvas known as Tramé, and it works best on Penelope canvas, where the yarn can be placed between the double threads of the canvas weft. This method improves coverage so that none of the white canvas can show through. It also serves to pad the stitches worked over it, making them fatter and thicker. It is sometimes used in order to create a slight rise in certain areas of the design for three-dimensional effect. Tramé is not used routinely because it adds to the time required to prepare the canvas.

Although painting the canvas makes it unnecessary to keep a color chart for your pattern close at hand, you will probably find that when you design your own canvas you have much less trouble remembering which colors go where. Since the design idea is your own, the color scheme comes naturally. And if you decide to change a color at the last minute, what does that matter?

A combination of pattern, color, and texture enhance the piano bench and lend emphasis to that section of the living room. Bargello combined with textural stitches. Worked by Suzanne Sheehan.

Chapter 9
Elements of Design

A pleasing design will automatically contain beauty, simplicity, and harmony among its parts. It will express a mood or a concept. Choosing subject matter for a design, putting the design elements together, selecting colors and textures, and then combining all these things within a defined area offer many possibilities for artistic originality.

Strangely, the essentials of good design are more conspicuous when they're missing than when they're present. To strengthen your perceptions of good versus faulty design, study designs from the past, those created by contemporary artists, and even those favored by commercial artists.

Your project's design should complement the purpose for which it's created. If you're covering a dining-room chair seat, lacy, open stitches will obviously be unsuitable. By the same token, heavy blocks of stitches would be out of place in a design for a box top.

The elements of good design include balance, proportion, scale, rhythm, dominance, and contrast.

These work together with space, line, form, pattern, texture, and color to create your statement. A pleasing design is just that — a statement of the artist's idea, whether the idea is a picture, a mood, or a motion. Even geometric patterns are a kind of statement; their language is balance and line.

Let's examine the elements of design one by one and see how they relate to needlepoint.

Balance can be called visual stability. It can be achieved through either symmetry or asymmetry. Symmetrical balance occurs when similar objects or shapes are placed on both sides of a vertical line that bisects the pattern. (The line is usually imaginary.) Thus, a rose centered on the left half of the pattern would be balanced symmetrically by a rose centered on the right half. This kind of balance is rather quiet and unobtrusive.

Asymmetrical balance is achieved through unequal or off-center distribution of visual weight. The asymmetry is balanced by the thoughtful use of color, line, size, and texture. Thus a large rose on the left side might be balanced by several smaller roses on the right. Asymmetrical balance is more pleasing aesthetically than symmetrical balance; it gives a pattern life and vigor.

Proportion has to do with the size relationship of the design to the total area of the project. One would not be likely to place a tiny mouse in the corner of a floor pillow, leaving the background unobtrusive and without strong design. By the same token, you'd hardly be tempted to work a design so large that it runs off the canvas before it is completed.

Scale also refers to relationships — those of each section of the design to all the other sections. To continue our absurd examples, a large mouse worked into a design with a tiny elephant would frighten more than the elephant.

Rhythm is created by the flow of lines and colors. These elements should create a subtle path that carries the viewer's eye along the design and confines it to the project, not allowing it to wander off the edge. The lines in good design tend toward a circular movement, forcing the eye back to the center and the predominant feature. A vase of gladiolas standing starkly upright with nary a bend or curve will be as unsatisfying in needlepoint design as it is in a floral arrangement. But add gently curved leaves, bend the stalks slightly, and place a small statue at the base and you'll have injected circular lines into the pattern to produce a pleasing motion.

Rhythm can also be achieved by repetition and by gradation. Exact repetition — the unvarying copying of other areas of a design — is monotonous and deadening. Better techniques are to change tint or texture, or to use smaller designs to balance the large design.

Dominance refers to the emphasis of one feature which becomes the main theme of your design. In an overall pattern of flowers, for instance, one flower is usually depicted whole and entire and therefore prominent among the rest. It need not necessarily be centered. Dominance implies the presence of subordination of other parts of the design. This can be achieved by varying size, shape, color, or texture.

Contrast is a technique for combining the elements of design in such a way as to emphasize their differences. Your placement of objects portrayed, of color, and of texture can create contrast within the total design. Thus, an overall flower pattern will include flowers of several sizes and shapes for contrast. Contrasting shapes and textures become especially important when you're using a monochromatic color scheme — one that uses several shades of a single basic color.

Chapter 10

Color

Color preference is a highly personal thing. Everyone sees colors in a slightly different way. Therefore, only general principles will be suggested here.

Since color affects emotions and can have an impact on the viewer's mood, the relationships among colors can play a vital role in the success of a project. An experienced needlepoint designer is always aware of color's role and respects it.

Stitches can look very different when worked in different colors. Pastel or light shades of any color add lights and shadows to a pattern that will make stitches look larger and more important. Dark colors have a tendency to retreat, making stitches look smaller, less distinct, and less significant.

Some colors create warmth and produce feelings of cheerfulness and excitement in the viewer. Such colors are mostly related to the sun — yellows, oranges, reds. They tend to reach out, to appear nearer and larger than other colors. An entire project done in warm colors may be exciting, but it can also be nervous in temperament.

Cool colors retreat and are restful. Greens, blues, and lavenders bring the grass and the sky to mind. A project done entirely in cool colors, however, can be dull and lethargic in its effect.

A combination of warm and cool colors will give balance and life to a project. A small touch of a warm color in a predominantly cool project enlivens the whole piece. When a project is overactive, touches of green and blue will tend to calm it down. Green and blue, being earth colors, also tend to blend with all other colors.

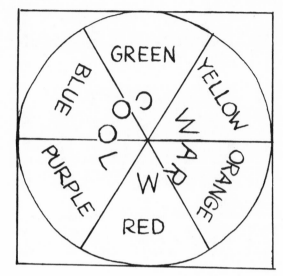

To learn more about colors, find yourself a good color wheel and study the families of colors it displays. The primary colors are red, yellow, and blue; they are basic colors, totally pure. When mixed together, they produce the secondary colors: red and yellow make orange; yellow and blue make green; blue and red make purple. When a primary and a secondary color are mixed, they make tertiary colors: Red-orange and yellow-orange; yellow-green and blue-green; blue-purple and red-purple.

Any color can be made lighter or darker by adding either white or black to it. In the red range, for example, there are a variety of colors from pink (red plus white) through primary red to dark red (red plus black). Such groupings are called "families" of colors. Each family is one color with all of its tints (additions of white) and shades (additions of black). Some authorities say families should never be mixed within a single project. But with careful attention to shading, I suggest you feel free to break that rule. Families cannot, it is true, be mixed with gay abandon. Yet some mixtures, especially among families of green, can add greatly to a total design.

Colors that are directly opposite each other on the color wheel offer exciting color schemes but should be used together with discretion. A small touch of red in an area of green emphasizes both, making the red redder and the green greener. But if you use these two colors in equal amounts, they tend to neutralize each other, and the result will leave the same impression on the viewer as a muddy brown. Not only does every pair of eyes see colors differently, but colors themselves can cause optical illusions.

There are several accepted terms for color combinations. I'll list them, just to let you know what you've already discovered, in all probability, through trial and error in a lifetime of seeing colors.

A *complementary color scheme* is made up of colors directly opposite each other on the color wheel. They can and should be used together, with consideration given to both the amount of each that you use and the tint or shade you choose. This sort of color scheme can be exciting and modern in the feeling it produces in the viewer.

A *split-complementary color scheme* combines a given color with the two colors lying on either side of its true complementary. Such a combination would, for example, include red, yellow-green, and blue-green. It produces the same feeling as complementaries.

A *triadic color scheme* combines three colors at equidistant points on the color wheel: Red, yellow, and blue, for instance, or orange, green, and purple. The same rules apply: don't use these colors in equal amounts of equivalent intensity. Such combinations can provide very rich harmonies.

A *tetrad* is built of four colors at four equidistant points of the wheel; it might include red, yellow-orange, green, and blue-violet.

Analogous color schemes use colors adjoining each other and all related to one primary color. These combinations are quite pleasing and relaxing, yet they have a strong emotional appeal.

A *monochromatic color scheme* sticks to a single color but employs the full range of its shades and tints. This scheme is restful and can be highly sophisticated, especially if you work in a variety of threads and textures.

A *multicolor scheme* goes all out, using every color, shade, and tint available. Such schemes give a feeling of fullness and richness. Here balance and arrangement of color must be given special thought and attention. If you let all the reds congregate on one side and all the blues on the other, you will have destroyed balance in the project.

The *rule of three* works well in achieving balanced color arrangements. Choose a predominant color for the project and use it in three areas, forming a triangle. Balance the triangle in the pattern design. The predominant color may be used further, in minute amounts (as on the tips of flowers or other very small areas), but it should be kept insignificant in feeling. Except in the predominant-color areas, it is used only for emphasis.

When you're selecting colors for a project, lay the threads in your hand in approximately the proportion each color will require. This will give you a good idea of how they'll look together. But keep in mind that a large hank of yarn will seem much more brilliant and intense than will the individual strands worked on canvas. You'll get a better idea of how colors blend, therefore, by approximating the amount of each color used than by picking up an indiscriminate handful of yarns.

Whenever you're selecting colors, do it in a good light. If you're trying to match upholstery material or other fabrics, it is essential that you see the colors in sunlight. Even the best artificial light will change color tones.

Design on right utilizes several pattern stitches; that on left is worked completely in Basketweave stitch. Notice contrast of texture and interest. (Work of Betty Sandock.)

Chapter 11

Texture

Pattern stitches give a design contrast by providing textural variations. Any project is enhanced by textural differences, even kits which call only for the Continental stitch. Texture changes will also alter the appearance and relationship of colors.

Too much texture will amount to overkill, however. It can cancel out the effects of each stitch, making the design seem too busy and therefore displeasing. In contemplating a balanced design, consider the contrast between "busy" and "quiet" stitches, between low and high stitches, and between large and small stitches. A textured background will often highlight a design worked in Basketweave or Continental stitch through contrasts of height, shadow, and size.

Each texture has its unique movement and characteristic; therefore each section of the design should be considered from the standpoint of importance and emphasis. Low, small stitches tend to fade away and retreat. Large, lumpy stitches — or those using more than one color — tend to intrude.

When choosing a stitch for any area, consider the

characteristics of each potential stitch in relation to the area it is to cover. Balance the size of the area with the size of the stitch. The directional line of a stitch may affect its suitability for an area; but don't be afraid to change the directional flow if it suits your purpose. Diagonal Mosaic, for instance, is normally worked top left to bottom right, but it doesn't have to be. Other considerations include whether the area to be covered is prominent or recessive, and what stitch will go next to it.

Stitches do not need to be the same size in every project. Just because the Sheaf stitch, for example, normally takes up four mesh, there is no reason it can't be enlarged to six or eight if such a texture is right for an area.

Basketweave and Continental should not be ignored in a wild burst of enthusiasm for texture. They should be considered as any other stitch, offering a smooth texture and often contrasting nicely with more flamboyant stitches. The idea is not to ignore the sedate stitches, but to keep them in their place and to use them in thoughtful ways.

It is an interesting exercise to work a project entirely in one color, possibly mixing threads, but relying entirely on texture — the pattern stitches — to bring out the design. The results can be quite sophisticated, even regal.

Chapter 12

Kits

I have been putting a good deal of emphasis on original design as opposed to needlepoint kits, but I am not ignoring the fact that many needleworkers like to do kits and may even prefer them. There are outstanding designers working in the field today. Should you find just what you like in a commercial canvas, you'll notice that a well-painted canvas is expensive. That's because time is expensive, and it takes time to cover each color boundary carefully with exactly the proper shade of color. In the best quality kits this is done by hand, and that's why such canvases are so expensive. Some silk-screen processes are quite good; silk-screened canvases constitute the middle range of prices. The less expensive kits have canvases prepared by more mechanical and complex methods of printing; they may or may not have the proper color marked where it's supposed to go, especially around the edges of the design.

If you're in doubt about whether the background color or the design color should be used in a given area of a commercial canvas, use this rule of thumb:

whichever color covers more than half of the intersection to be covered wins. In practice, it may take some trial and error before you reach a satisfying decision.

On any canvas — and this advice applies even more to hand-painted than to mechanically printed ones — test for color stability before starting in to work. If there's any doubt about the permanence of the color, treat the canvas with clear acrylic spray.

Some kits come with an unmarked piece of canvas; the design is printed on a separate sheet of graph paper. Such kits are interesting to work; they are very precise in letting you know which color goes where. Each square on the graph paper represents one stitch on your canvas. A marking code signifies the colors to use. Thus three code marks representing yellow in three squares of the graph tell you there should be three yellow stitches applied to the canvas.

To begin working a graphed design, find the exact center of the design and the exact center of the canvas and start there. Work either in one direction or around in more or less a circle, depending on the design. A color can be taken across several empty holes to fill in a nearby spot, but limit this technique to areas no more than an inch apart. Later stitches will cover the yarn on the back. If other stitches have already been worked between nearby areas of one color, run the yarn under them so it won't be loose on the back of the project. Loose threads tend to catch.

It's sometimes very helpful to mark the canvas,

before beginning a design, by drawing vertical and horizontal lines with a waterproof marking pen to divide the canvas into quarters. Then mark every tenth mesh in each direction on these lines. Since the graph paper is also marked every ten squares, you'll have a guideline on the canvas to help you locate areas more easily.

part

IV

Innovative Techniques

Chapter 13

Free Your Imagination

Various threads and methods used: Heavy wire, jewel, cordé thread, cloisonné silver, DMC floss, knitting yarn, cut work, needleweaving, appliqué.

For years, even centuries, needlepoint was in bondage to the Tent stitch and its variations, with the pattern stitches being employed only on rare occasions. As recently as a decade ago, few needleworkers considered using anything but the Tent stitch — and that on a design already worked when the kit was purchased. We've come a long way in ten years.

If we can return to the ancient concept of needlepoint as one category of needlework, it will help to liberate needlework from its confining pigeonholes among the fiber arts and their techniques. Such an approach will free needleworkers' imaginations from the tight little preconceived notions that hedged them in for too many years. It will free the craft of needlepoint to become truly the art of needlepoint, and it will mean that centuries from now archaeologists will be able to identify the work of this era as distinctly our work, the needlepoint of the late twentieth century.

To liberate needlepoint, we must think of needlepoint canvas as being a ground for design — as linen is to embroidery, as burlap is to rug hooking, as string, jute, and hemp are to macramé. With that frame of mind, there will be no limit to our creativity. Such a point of view does away with "needlepoint stitches," "crewel stitches," and "embroidery stitches." There are only stitches, to be used wherever and whenever they achieve the effects we seek. Effects once considered specific to other fabric arts are just as achievable in needlepoint. Often each effect is worked differently in the different media and called by different names, but the appearance is the same, whatever the medium. For example, the Chain stitch is worked in weaving by using the fingers; in crochet, by using a hook; in embroidery, with a needle — but they are all distinctly Chain stitches.

If we can forget which yarns and methods are "traditional" to needlepoint and borrow methods from other fabric arts to create new statements in needlepoint, we will be accepting our responsibility to those who come after us in the field. There is no standing still in the arts; either we forge ahead and break new ground or we become frozen in the past, condemned to repeat it slavishly and unimaginatively.

One of the preconceptions needlepoint artists should rid themselves of is that needlepoint has to be two-dimensional. In fact, it need not be flat. Two canvases can be combined to form a three-dimensional work (known as appliqué; more about that in Chapter 14). Jewels, mirrors, or stones can be added

The basket was worked separately and applied on three sides to form a realistic basket.

to a project to achieve naturalistic effects. Threads not ordinarily associated with needlepoint can be introduced when we realize that not all threads need to be incorporated through the canvas — some can be attached to the top by means of another thread. If a desired technique is more easily worked using a nontraditional method, there is no reason not to incorporate it onto your canvas.

In short, whatever expresses your concept and enhances your project is acceptable. The only limit is good design. Simplicity, to repeat, is the sole concern. Each movement of the design must make its own statement in relationship to other sections of the total design, and care should be taken that no section overpowers another. As in color choice, the innovations should complement one another, and the overall feeling of the work must "fit." Hemp accents on a silk purse obviously are incongruous. But hemp used on a coarse beach scene, along with pebbles, sea shells, and a general feeling of the sea, can be delightful.

Let's look more closely at some of these ideas.

Chapter 14

Appliqué

To appliqué is to apply one piece of material to another.

"Material," in this case, can be anything: another piece of canvas, a stone, a flower, a sea shell, a jewel, a piece of lace — anything that cannot be pulled through the holes of the canvas as yarn is.

There are several ways of attaching such "foreign" objects to the canvas, depending largely upon the object.

One method of attaching one piece of canvas to another is "layering." If part of your project is a minute, highly detailed section of design, you may prefer to work it on a piece of petit point and then apply the section to the larger-mesh canvas on which background is to be worked. Depending on the complexity of your project, this process can be repeated more than once.

You can create pockets in your design (as in the balloons photograph) by finishing one edge of the small piece with a binding stitch and then appliquéing it to the canvas before the background is worked.

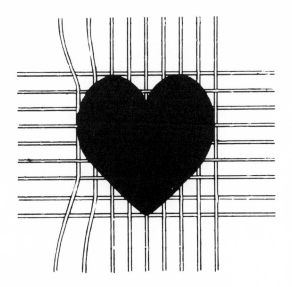

To appliqué a piece of worked canvas to a background, ravel unworked portion of appliqué and pull freed threads through background canvas.

Threads are pulled to the back of the canvas and fastened down. Then both layers of canvas are worked simultaneously.

To appliqué two pieces of canvas together, work the petit point or other piece to be appliquéd fully, leaving at least an inch and a half of unworked canvas all around. Next unweave the excess canvas, being cautious near the worked area not to pull any threads out from under the yarn. Lay this worked canvas on top of the blank canvas and pull each raveled thread through the background canvas; often this is most easily done with a large-eye needle, although a very fine crochet hook can also be used. When all the threads have been pulled through to the back of the main canvas, smooth them down and stitch the ends to the main canvas with sewing thread. Now work the background up to the appliqué over the threads of both canvases, and the appliqué will be held securely in place.

This method produces a flat appliqué. For a three-

An interpretation of a memory of Pine Mountain, Ky. The butterfly floats freely over rock and flowers. (Work of the author.)

dimensional effect, the appliqué design is worked completely, using the Basketweave or some other small-pattern stitch. Then carefully cut out the appliqué design right up to the wool. Paint the back of the piece with clear nail polish and allow it to dry. Now work Buttonhole stitches all around the edges of the appliqué piece and attach the piece to the background canvas with whatever stitch suits the mood of the overall design. For example, the butterfly in the "Pine Mountain" photograph was attached by using the Satin stitch for the body through both canvases. French knots or Turkey stitch make useful as well as lovely flower centers. Any stitch will do so long as it's in keeping with the design. Pellon ironed on the back of the appliqué piece gives it some stiffness and stability and will keep it pointed out from the main canvas if that's your objective.

Stump work, popular in the seventeenth century and again during the Victorian era, offers another method for three-dimensional work. Stump work consists of layering two pieces of material together with padding. It differs from quilting in that only the design is padded, filling it out to a rounded shape. In other times, stump work was used primarily for human figures and animals.

Stump work can be useful in needlepoint for adding depth and texture. The section to be padded is worked separately, then appliquéd to the background with a pad of cotton placed between the background and the design.

Stones, jewels, sea shells, and other unusual items can be attached to the canvas. Use any method that will make them stay where they're supposed to be, including glue, crewel stitches, or invisible thread.

"Cupping" the object — surrounding it with small Buttonhole stitches built on themselves — is useful for holding jewels and odd-shaped objects firmly. Begin by daubing a touch of glue on the object to anchor it to the canvas. Then, holding the object to the canvas with a free thumb, work around the object with small back stitches. Leave them quite loose. After the object is surrounded, begin making Buttonhole stitches into each back stitch. Build the Buttonhole stitches row-on-row, pulling each row tighter until the object is hugged firmly to the canvas. This procedure works with jewels, shells, glass, or any three-dimensional object. Normally the canvas is worked before such objects are applied.

Shisha glass — small mirrors typically used in the needlework of the provinces of Kutch, Kathiawan, and Sind in Western India — adds sparkle and grandeur to a design. "Mylar," a mirrorlike aluminum material backed with linen or cotton, which is easily obtained at most art shops, makes an acceptable and accessible form of shisha glass. It can be cut into desired shapes. These mirrors are normally laid down by crosshatching threads, first across the top and bottom, then along both sides. Next place four more threads at angles to the first four, covering the edges of the glass entirely. Finally, lace small Buttonhole stitches into these threads and anchor them in the material to hold the threads away from the center of the glass and fix the Mylar firmly in place. This

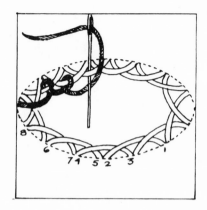

Cupping

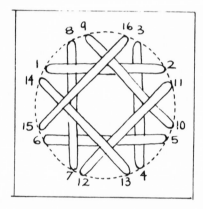

Shisha A

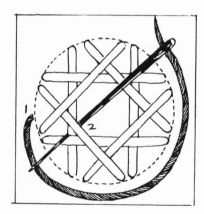

Shisha B

150

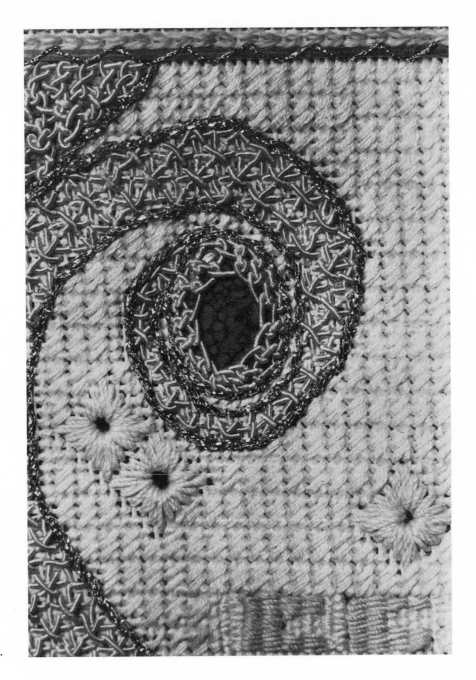

A grafted design.

is the traditional method, but any arrangement of threads which holds the glass to the canvas and allows the glitter to be seen is acceptable. As with jewels, stones, and the like, the background is usually worked first.

Sequins and beads can be used to highlight special features of a design. They can represent dew on a leaf, drops of water, the sparkle of the sun, the eyes of an animal, and anything else your creativity suggests. They are normally sewn on top of a finished canvas. Invisible thread is especially useful for securing beads. Sequins can be held with a French knot or a small bead sewn in the center for a solid anchor.

Invisible thread is made of transparent nylon filaments and is useful in countless ways. It comes in "black" or "white" — actually dark or light filaments, since there is virtually no color in the thread. When it's sewn, such thread is absolutely invisible, making it ideal for stitching down almost anything that shouldn't appear obviously sewn. It is also good for tacking cording or braiding onto the edges of pillows. Use invisible thread whenever you want the method of stitching to remain a secret.

As an alternative, however, lace and cord can be stitched down by "couching" them with other stitches. Couching is simply a process of using one thread to tack down another to the background material. Only the couching thread goes through the canvas. This technique is most often used with gold cord; the robes of ancient China were heavily laden with couched gold cord. For needlepoint purposes,

The center band of lace is blind-stitched with invisible thread. The lace at top and bottom is couched on with Herringbone stitch.

many stitches may be used in attaching one thread to another. The Herringbone stitch, sewn loosely, creates a lovely braid effect. The Chain stitch, the open Buttonhole, and many of the "crewel stitches" may be used. Straight stitches applied in a measured manner create patterns in themselves.

154

Half "embroidery stitches" and half "needlepoint stitches": needlepoint includes Eyelet, Gobelin, Laced Scotch, Brick, Sheaf; embroidery includes Alternating Stem, Buttonhole, Portuguese Stem, Chain.

Chapter 15

Borrowed Stitches

To send your imagination really soaring, consider the canvas not as a challenge to be filled completely but as a background material on which to create. Among the most useful tools available to the creative needlepointer are the stitches known as "embroidery stitches," which highlight and give textural balance to a design.

Terms like "embroidery stitch" and "needlepoint stitch" are really misnomers. Embroidery stitches are just as much at home on canvas as needlepoint stitches are at home on linen. It is the passion of the twentieth century to categorize; in this case, categorizing has limited needleworkers within unnecessarily confining boundaries.

Any embroidery stitch may be used on canvas. Combined with needlepoint stitches, they provide exciting opportunities for emphasis in a design. Outlining areas with the Chain stitch, for example, delineates the shapes. The Satin stitch, the Long-and-Short stitch, and the Roumanian stitch help to ease problems of shading.

There will be times when you find the textural quality of an embroidery stitch more desirable than anything a needlepoint stitch can furnish. Suppose you're working a tree trunk; the Outline stitch results in far more lifelike texture and easier shading than the Tent stitch or any pattern stitch. Or perhaps you're doing a lamb; he'll look much woolier done with French knots than with a smoother-textured stitch.

Combining crewel stitches with a needlepoint background can produce a three-dimensional effect. Crewel flowers particularly tend to stand out from a background. The combination of crewel and needlepoint stitches, sometimes called crewelpoint, also adds an extra dimension to texture. When combining these two kinds of stitches, you'll find it simpler to work the crewel design first and needlepoint around it afterward. If the needlepoint stitch proves not to fit perfectly, an area of Tent stitches surrounding the design will not look out of place.

"Creweled" birds and tree branch add a third dimension to Basketweave background.

Chapter 16

Needleweaving

The same elements and techniques used in drawn work on linen carry over nicely to needlepoint. Threads may be cut and drawn from a canvas just as they are from linen. The process leaves an area of warp or weft threads which can then be bound together for a lacy effect.

In needleweaving, a filling (horizontal) thread is woven around, under, and over long warp (vertical) threads to form patterns. Weft (horizontal) threads in the canvas may be cut and drawn out, leaving the warp threads as the basis for the needleweaving. Alternatively, fresh warp threads may be laid over worked canvas to provide the needleweaving base.

The weaving techniques are the same as those used in loom weaving: Over a thread, under a thread. Whether this rhythm is carried across the entire width of canvas or applied only to groups of two or three threads at a time depends on the results desired. Lovely patterns can be built up by "wrapping" several threads for a short distance and then changing to a new set of threads. The unwrapped

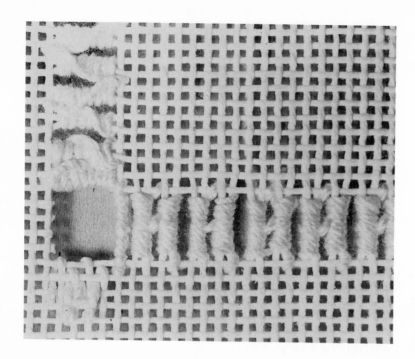

Four threads have been removed and the remaining threads have been woven in patterns.

threads are then covered with Buttonhole stitches to give them a finished appearance. (As an example of how the fiber arts are related, this Buttonhole stitch would be called the Half-Hitch in macramé.)

Large areas can be made very lacy by cutting out threads in one direction and weaving a pattern on the remaining threads. First determine the area to be opened; then cut the threads in the center of the area and gently unravel them to the border of the area. Thread each thread on a needle and weave it back through the canvas to anchor it firmly. The background around the area will be worked over the double threads, hiding them and giving security to the cut section.

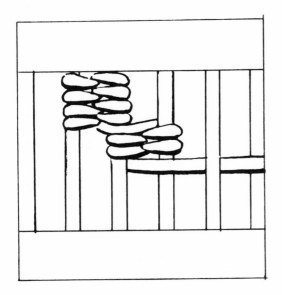

Needleweaving

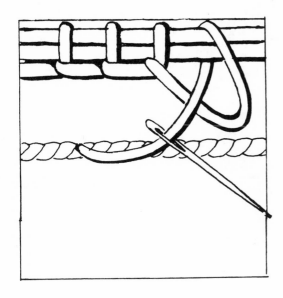

Needleweaving

To work the open area, select a set of warp threads and begin weaving over and under, around the end, and over and under again. For diversion, two threads can be counted as one; thus, over two, under two. If the selected pairs of threads are changed at the beginning of every new row, the result will be a brick effect — or "twill," as it is called in weaving.

If there is to be no cutout area, long warp threads can be laid on top of the worked canvas and used as a basis for needleweaving. This, too, will produce a three-dimensional effect.

Using the same method but doing it backwards, as in three-dimensional appliqué, involves cutting areas out of the canvas entirely. This leaves an opening through which something else shows from behind — a jewel, a piece of cloth, a separate scene. To achieve the cutout, bravely snip the area from the canvas. Paint the edges of the cutout area with clear nail polish and let it dry. Then finish the edge with a Buttonhole stitch that covers at least two holes into the canvas for safety. (The combination of nail polish and stitches will keep the edges from raveling.) The Buttonhole legs into the canvas can be worked over and covered when the area around the hole is being done.

Threads can be run across the opening, if desired, and worked by needleweaving. Or a smaller design can be worked on canvas, finished as with appliqué, and then applied to the cutout area with threads which are then covered with Buttonhole stitches for a finished look.

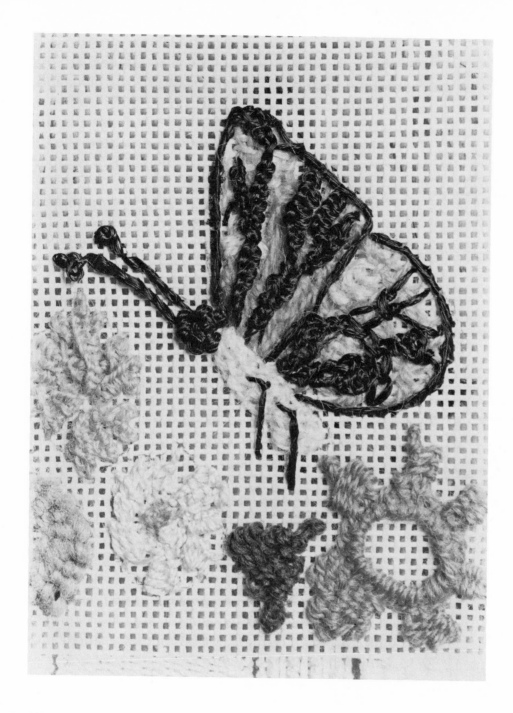

right

Adaptation of Victorian cut-work pattern. Parts of wings have been cut out and threads needlewoven across. Some crewel stitches provide highlights.

left

Extra threads have been laid on top of canvas and then used as base for needle-weaving.

Fabric may be placed behind the hole, or you can hang objects like rings or bells in the open area. The only criterion for such projects is that the hole have a meaning in the overall pattern of the project.

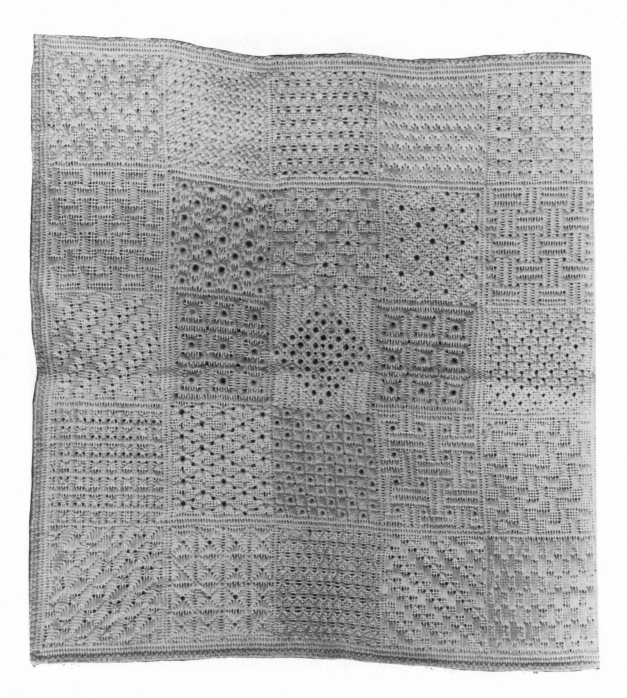

Chapter 17

Pulled Work

When Colonial women worked their men's pocketbooks, they sometimes used the "Queen's stitch." It gave a dainty appearance and also worked well for the kind of project at hand.

The Queen's stitch is really the Rococo stitch pulled tight at the four outer corners. A needle or skewer is used first to enlarge the four corner-holes; then the tension of the stitch is worked more tightly than usual. This pulls the canvas out of line and produces open holes in the work. Since Rococo is best worked on the diagonal, Queen's stitch designs tend to have a diamond, or zig-zag, pattern.

Other stitches offer similar possibilities for "pulled work," as this technique is called. Three very compatible ones are the Algerian Eye, Diamond Eyelet, and Satin stitches. All that's necessary is unlocked canvas and exceptional tension when working. The technique is particularly attractive when used with thin yarn that doesn't cover — crochet cotton, for instance, or perle cotton, silk, or floss. The tension of the stitch will result in smaller, daintier holes. If larger holes are desired, a needle or skewer can be used first to move the canvas threads apart.

Matching the yarn to the canvas (or dyeing the canvas to match the yarn) results in an elegant appearance with this technique, emphasizing only the stitch formation. When various colors are used in the thread, the emphasis shifts to the colors from the light/shadow pattern of the stitches.

You must be careful about even tension and the placement of the next stitch with pulled work. Uneven tension results in thick and thin lines and uneven holes which destroy the dainty feeling that is your goal in this sort of work. Where the next stitch is to begin determines the lie of the thread from the last stitch, affecting the tension on the hole. Each stitch must pull back the thread from the previous stitch, opening the hole evenly. Because so much canvas is left showing, or because of the holes resulting in tight tension, you must take the thread from one area to the next behind the canvas threads.

Leaving some of the canvas showing adds to the lace effect. Note that a different mental attitude is required for working in pulled work. While the finished project looks as though a breath would destroy it, the project is really quite strong and long-wearing.

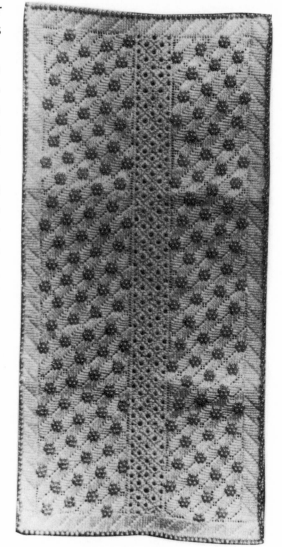

Chapter 18
Simplicity

The fundamental goal in striving for a perfect design is to find ways to express a concept in the most simple, straightforward way possible. Good design is always simple, with all its parts coming together to make a unified whole. You will learn how to select the best means for expressing your concept through experience, open-mindedness to "borrowed" techniques, willingness to experiment, and a certain exuberant joy of expression that is hard to define but gives life and individuality to your designs.

Knowing what to delete is as important in creating a design as knowing what to include. Good designers also learn to take failures in stride. Not every idea works out, but one can learn as much from mistakes as from successes — and sometimes more. Each project you do will add to your experience and self-confidence. I sometimes think that a really good needlepoint artist deserves a Ph.D. in "ripping out."

Perhaps there ought to be a caution printed on the packages needlepoint materials come in. Something like "Warning: Needlepoint Is Addictive." I certainly find needlepoint addictive; there's always one more row to do, one more project keeping my mind a trifle ill at ease until I've mastered the challenge it offers. But unlike a good many other addictions, needlepoint isn't hazardous to your health, and it doesn't make you fat or turn you into an unpleasant person.

There are side benefits to needlepoint that enhance its attractiveness. Deep friendships can begin with an exchange of stitch patterns or project ideas. Hands busy with stitching won't be in the cookie jar. And minds dulled by lethargy or stunned by too much time watching the TV set can be restored to life with new ideas and anticipations.

"And all because my lady wife has taken to embroider!"

Bibliography
and
Source List

Bibliography

Alderson, Chottie. *Advanced Canvaswork Course.* Running Springs, Cal.: Embroiderers' Guild of America, 1974.

Baker, Muriel; Eyre, Barbara; Wall, Margaret; and Westerfield, Charlotte. *Needlepoint: Design Your Own.* New York: Scribners, 1974.

Baker, Muriel L. *The ABC's of Canvas Embroidery.* Old Sturbridge Village, Mass.: Old Sturbridge Village Booklet Series, 1968.

———. *The XYZ's of Canvas Embroidery.* Old Sturbridge Village, Mass.: Old Sturbridge Village Booklet Series, 1972.

Cirker, Blanche, ed. *Needlework Alphabets and Designs.* New York: Dover Publications, 1975.

Enthoven, Jacqueline. *The Stitches of Creative Embroidery.* New York: Van Nostrand Reinhold, 1964.

Fischer, Pauline, and Lasker, Anabel. *Bargello Magic.* New York: Holt, Rinehart & Winston, 1972.

Hanley, Hope. *Needlepoint.* 2nd edition. New York: Scribners, 1975.

Ireys, Katherine. *Finishing and Mounting Your Needlepoint Pieces.* New York: Thomas Y. Crowell, 1973.

Kaestner, Dorothy. *Four Way Bargello.* New York: Scribners, 1972.

Katzenberg, Gloria. *Art and Stitchery: New Directions.* New York: Scribners, 1974.

Lantz, Sherlee, with diagrams by Maggie Lane. *A Pageant of Pattern for Needlepoint Canvas.* New York: Atheneum, 1973.

Nordfors, Jill. *Needle Lace and Needleweaving.* New York: Van Nostrand Reinhold, 1974.

Rhodes, Mary. *Needlepoint: The Art of Canvas Embroidery.* London: Octopus Books, Ltd., 1974.

Rome, Carol Cheney, and Devlin, Georgia French. *A New Look at Needlepoint: The Complete Guide to Canvas Embroidery.* New York: Crown Publishers, 1972.

Weal, Michele. *Texture and Color in Needlepoint.* New York: Harper & Row, 1975.

Williams, Elsa S. *Creative Canvas Work.* New York: Van Nostrand Reinhold, 1974.

———. *Bargello: Florentine Canvas Work.* New York: Van Nostrand Reinhold, 1967.

Wilson, Erica. *Erica Wilson's Embroidery.* New York: Scribners, 1973.

Source List

Schoolhouse Two, 100 Center, Mishawaka, Ind. 46544
(yarn caddies).

Erica's, 1602½ Mishawaka Ave., South Bend, Ind. 46615
(Needle Ease frames).

Frederick J. Fawcett, Inc., 129 South St., Boston, Mass. 02111,
(linen yarns).

Dirl's, P.O. Box 1499, Covina, Cal. 91722
(floor frames).

The Designing Woman, Lakeville, Conn. 06039
(original designs, materials).

DMC Corp., 107 Trumbull St., Elizabeth, N.J. 07206
(threads, materials, patterns).

Dee Needlepoint Originals, P.O. Box 1756, Pt. Pleasant Beach, N.J. 08742
(markers, all supplies, special graph notebooks).

Peacock Alley, 652 Croswell, S.E., Grand Rapids, Mich. 49506
(original designs).

Magic Needle, 44 Green Bay Rd., Winnetka, Ill. 60093
(original designs).

Needle Arts, Inc., 28 Washington St., Camden, Me. 04843
(original designs, accessories, supplies).

Nantucket Needleworks, Nantucket Island, Mass. 02554
(outstanding colors of yarn, all supplies, original designs).

Needle Ease, 81 Uplands Dr., West Hartford, Conn. 06107
(lap frames, frame easels).